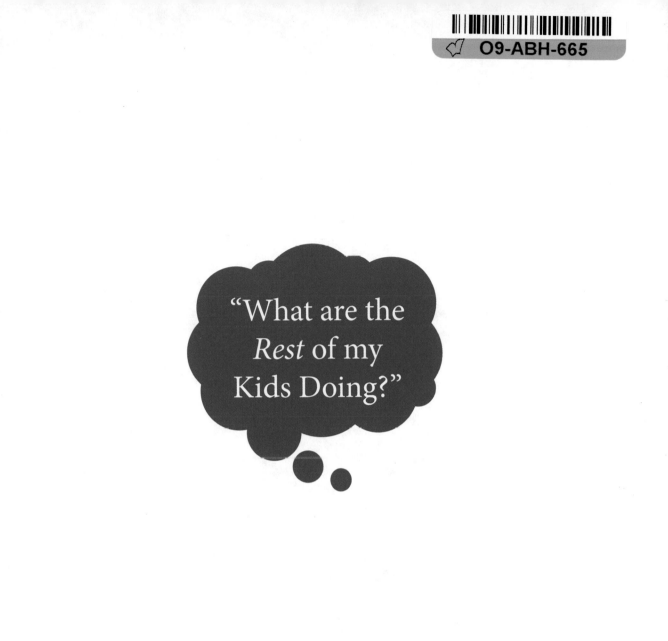

Lindsey Moses with MERIDITH OGDEN

"What are the Rest of my Kids Doing?"

Fostering Independence in the K–2 Reading Workshop

HEINEMANN
Portsmouth, NH

Heinemann

361 Hanover Street

Portsmouth, NH 03801–3912

www.heinemann.com

Offices and agents throughout the world

Library of Congress Cataloging-in-Publication Data
Names: Moses, Lindsey, author. | Ogden, Meridith, collaborator.
Title: What are the rest of my kids doing? : fostering independence in the K–2 reading workshop / by Lindsey Moses, with Meridith Ogden.
Description: Portsmouth, NH : Heinemann, [2017]
Identifiers: LCCN 2016046000| ISBN 9780325087757
| ISBN 9780325092645 | ISBN 9780325092652
Subjects: LCSH: Reading (Primary)—United States. | Reading comprehension—Study and teaching—United States.
Classification: LCC LB1525 .M74 2017 | DDC 372.40973—dc23
LC record available at https://lccn.loc.gov/2016046000

Editor: Holly Kim Price
Production editor: Sonja S. Chapman
Cover and interior designs: Suzanne Heiser
Typesetter: Shawn Girsberger
Manufacturing: Steve Bernier

Printed in the United States of America on acid-free paper

21   20   19   18   17   VP   2   3   4   5

Lindsey

For Adela and Mikaela, I hope your primary

years are filled with teachers like Meridith who

nurture a love for reading, thinking,

and exploring.

Meridith

For my first graders, you are the heart and soul

of this book, and without you it would not

have been possible.

Contents

Acknowledgments

LINDSEY

So many people deserve thanks and acknowledgement for their contributions to this book. First and foremost, my coauthor, Meridith Ogden, thank you for allowing me to be part of your classroom to learn alongside you and your amazing first graders for two years. You are an inspirational teacher who changes the lives of so many students. Two years of video recording, researching, refining, and writing this book were possible because of the children and families at Cactus View Elementary and Pinnacle Peak Elementary.

I would like to especially thank Michelle Flynn, Cathy Brophy, and the Heinemann PD staff for opportunities to work with amazing schools and teachers over the last six years. This book was inspired by the question I frequently heard when providing PD: "But what are the rest of the kids doing while I am pulling small groups or conferring?" I am so thankful for the opportunity to have worked with teachers and schools to create spaces where children can develop independence and a love of reading. A special thanks to Baltimore County Public Schools and Martin County School District, which helped me see a need for this book. Our long-term work together helped me articulate the process of facilitating meaningful literacy independence.

A big thanks to our editor, Holly Kim Price, for her guidance, feedback, support, and conversations from the initial idea through the final product. I would also like to thank the great team at Heinemann who helped make this book possible: Sarah Fournier, Amanda Bondi, and members of the editorial, marketing, and production teams.

Thank you to Laura Beth Kelly. I couldn't have asked for a better research assistant to be part of that first year in Meridith's classroom.

To my parents, Karen and Mike, thank you. Your respect for and commitment to education was contagious.

Finally, I would like to thank Frank Serafini. Thank you for your unwavering belief in me. Your endless encouragement and support have made me a better teacher, researcher, and partner. I am so thankful to have you in my life.

MERIDITH

Great teachers challenge our thinking, encourage us to reach beyond what we feel is attainable, and guide us along our journey with kindness and respect. Lindsey, thank you for being my greatest teacher, true friend, and coauthor. Our time together in the classroom has truly changed my practice and because of you I have a deeper sense of self. To my students: your minds are beautiful and your thoughts are worth sharing. Thank you for always letting me listen in and falling in love with books alongside me. I am grateful for my administrator who trusted my passion and my colleagues who shared the passion. Finally, for Ryan, although you may not always understand the art of teaching, you understand, respect, and support my journey as an educator, and for that I love you.

1 · Foundations for Independence in the K–2 Reading Workshop

Lindsey has had the privilege of working with teachers and schools across the country on finding ways to support all *learners during reading and writing instruction. As many schools move to a more student-centered, differentiated instructional support model, one challenge teachers face is creating meaningful learning experiences for the class while they are conferring or working with small groups. The question she hears most frequently is, "Yes, but what are all the other kids doing?" As teachers focus on conferences or small groups for needs-based instruction, unfortunately, they often give busywork to other students to diminish interruptions. Even in classrooms that claim to be running a workshop model, teachers often feel guilty about what is being accomplished while they are providing focused small-group and individual instruction. Many teachers have tried different options including silent reading, reading response journals, worksheets, centers, independent work, computer time, spelling work, word work, a combination of these, or the "must do, may do" list of options. However, Lindsey frequently hears frustrations with the lack of meaningful work or productivity that takes place when students are working independently.*

Many of Lindsey's professional development workshops address the topic of providing purposeful independent learning experiences for students. In these experiences, the teacher introduces learning opportunities that allow children to engage with authentic texts in meaningful ways without the teacher. Intermediate-grade students are more comfortable with this because in general they are more independent and can read, write, and work for greater lengths of time without the teacher. However, primary-grade teachers often voice the following concerns:

- *The students can't read independently yet.*
- *The students can't remain quiet for longer than 5–10 minutes.*
- *The students can't write independently yet.*
- *For the students to be learning, they need instruction/interaction from adults.*

- *They need to be practicing skills.*
- *They have trouble being independent decision makers and knowing how to manage their time and what to do next.*

Although these are all valid concerns, there are ways to foster independence in a classroom environment. In addition to conducting research and professional development in classrooms and schools across the country, Lindsey spent a year with an outstanding first-grade teacher, Meridith, in Arizona. Meridith was teaching in a Title I first-grade classroom with a diverse group of twenty-eight students (no, that is not a typo; the capacity in first grade in Arizona is thirty students). We wanted our readers to enjoy reading and independently engage with a wide variety of texts in meaningful ways. To do this, we knew we had to introduce and facilitate purposeful independent opportunities for students to practice and apply their new literacy knowledge. As anyone who has taught in the primary grades knows, this is much easier said than done. So, we set out to document the process of facilitating independence through weekly video recordings, photography, and planning sessions over the course of a year.

We believe strongly that all instruction should be deeply rooted in the following areas: research, theory, experience, and most importantly, the ever-changing young children in our classrooms.

• What Do We Believe?

Drawing on the theorists, scholars, and educators that came before us, we believe in student-centered and inquiry approaches to teaching and learning (Dewey 1997; Wells 1999). Sociocultural perspectives on literacy shape our thinking about learning in context. We agree with Vygotsky's (1978) theory that development must be considered in relation to historical, social, and cultural contexts and that individual development depends on language and interactions with others. Essentially, learning is a socially based activity. So, what does this have to do with fostering independence? A lot! Students must engage in interactions with adults and peers to support their development toward independence. It is only through meaningful and contextualized experiences surrounding literacy that young children develop the motivation and competence to engage independently. This then leads to additional opportunities to engage with adults and peers, as the cycle of development and independence progresses and becomes more sophisticated in nature. We believe supporting independence must be grounded in the children, and there is no prescribed approach for all young children. Because of this, all of our instruction arose from initial observations and interactions with students.

• What Does Early Literacy Research Say?

A large focus has been placed on early literacy development and performance in the last fifteen years. A goal of No Child Left Behind legislation in 2001 was to have all students reading on grade level by third grade. This led to a large focus on the five pillars of literacy: phonics, phonological awareness, vocabulary, comprehension, and fluency. Although each of these aspects of literacy is important, they don't all carry the same weight. As Duke and Block (2012) note, "Measurable gains in phonological awareness, alphabet knowledge and word reading can be achieved quickly, and for most students, relatively easily. In contrast, gains in comprehension, vocabulary, and conceptual knowledge are harder to measure, at least in young children, and harder to achieve" (66). Failing to support these areas has been documented to have long-term consequences in student learning. Because of this, we utilize small groups and conferring to support and address the specific needs of individual students instead of using a predetermined whole-class scope and sequence of phonics- and skills-based instruction. Students develop independence when they work on skills and construct meaning with self-selected texts.

Students in classrooms where teachers emphasize high-level thinking and talking with strategies such as making connections, identifying themes, and making inferences about characters show significant gains, even in low-income settings (Taylor, Frye, and Maruyama 1990). With the Common Core State Standards (National Governors Association Center for Best Practices and Council of Chief

State School Officers 2010b) and implementation of state-level college- and career-readiness standards, greater demands and expectations are being placed on children in the early grades.

To maximize progression for beginning readers, teachers must make sure students are engaged in meaningful literacy activities during the entire literacy period. This does *not* mean the teacher should be providing instruction the majority of the time (ask yourself, "Who is doing the work?"). We encourage minilessons to support whole-group needs, but the majority of the literacy period should allow for students to be "doing the work" of reading, thinking, and discussing. Their independent learning experiences must be purposeful and beneficial to their development because the bulk of their literacy time will be spent without direct interaction with the teacher. To support students in becoming independent, confident, and competent, we have to understand the development progression of young learners.

• Progression of Literacy Development

There are a variety of ways to discuss the stages of literacy development. Fountas and Pinnell (2011) developed a continuum of literacy learning with corresponding leveled text. Others use Lexile levels, Developmental Reading Assessment (DRA) levels, Dynamic Indicators of Basic Early Literacy Skills (DIBELS) scores, grade-level expectations, or various norm-referenced assessments. Although we, too, assess reading performance of our young learners using these tools, we also find that a more general understanding of literacy progression helps to inform decisions we make about developmentally appropriate practice. The National Association of the Education of Young Children (NAEYC) and International Reading Association (IRA) identify phases in a continuum of early reading and writing (1998).

Based on this understanding, IRA and NAEYC recommend effective reading instruction for kindergarten and primary grades that includes but is not limited to the following:

- reading meaningful and engaging stories and informational text daily
- giving students opportunities to independently read meaningful and engaging stories and informational text daily
- providing balanced literacy instruction that includes decoding and meaningful reading instruction
- establishing opportunities for small groups that provide focused instruction and collaboration with other students
- teaching a curriculum that is intellectually engaging and challenging to expand children's knowledge of the world and develop vocabulary

These instructional suggestions are the beginning steps in creating an environment that fosters independence among young learners in the reading workshop.

	Children can . . .
Phase 2 (kindergarten)	· Listen to stories and retell simple narrative stories or informational text · Use expressive language to describe and explore · Recognize and name letters · Demonstrate letter-sound correspondence · Demonstrate some recognition of rhyme and beginning sounds · Understand basic print concepts (read left to right, top to bottom) · Match printed words with spoken words
Phase 3 (first grade)	· Read and retell familiar stories · Use strategies (rereading, predicting, questioning, contextualizing) when comprehension breaks down · Use reading and writing for various purposes on their own initiative · Orally read with reasonable fluency · Use letter-sound associations, word parts, and context to identify new words · Identify an increasing number of words by sight
Phase 4 (second grade)	· Read with greater fluency · Use strategies more efficiently when comprehension breaks down · Use word identification strategies with greater facility to identify unknown words · Identify an increasing number of words by sight

Figure 1.1 Expected reading development

Figure 1.1 shows an adaptation of expected reading development for children in the primary grades (phases 2, 3, and 4) from the IRA and NAEYC (1998, 15–16).

• Young Learners and the Reading Workshop

Reading workshop experts and scholars have addressed multiple ways to create a student-centered framework for teaching and learning (Calkins 2010; Moses 2015; Serafini 2001; Serravallo 2010; Taberski 2000). Although they all have slightly different takes on the implementation, schedules, and logistics, there is a general consensus about essential components and learning opportunities. They all agree that on most days children should engage in a brief, teacher-guided lesson (also referred to as a minilesson), independent reading (and/or responding) with choice, small-group opportunities, conferring, and sharing.

We utilize a workshop approach to our instruction, but have adapted it to foster meaningful independence among young readers. We begin by observing young readers to identify additional scaffolds that will deepen their independent learning experiences. The goal is not for students to demonstrate strategies, skills, silent reading, and specific behaviors. Instead, our goal is independence. We follow steps for building stamina in the beginning of the year, but we feel like the students need more. It isn't as simple as introducing expectations, practicing it for a week, and then expecting students' independent time to be meaningful. This is why we spend a year on developing independence with young readers and documenting it. Most of the routines, structures, strategies, and learning opportunities have to not only be introduced but revisited to extend and deepen their experiences.

Purposeful Learning Experiences Foster Independence

Lindsey started using the term *purposeful learning experiences* (PLEs) when referring to what the other kids should be doing. Many schools develop routines to keep students busy or quiet so teachers could confer and run small groups. However, primary teachers in particular worried about the quality and value of what students were doing to keep busy during the bulk of their literacy block. Their reflexivity about this was impressive, and Lindsey suggested they ask themselves if the quiet work had a purpose or enhanced *literacy development* (not behavior management). She told them to review every center, every routine, every worksheet (hopefully, not many), every response opportunity, and ask themselves, "What purpose does this serve in my students' literacy development?" If it doesn't serve a valid purpose, throw it out. To make this shift, we had to identify what PLEs are and what they are not (see Figure 1.2).

PLEs are not	PLEs could be
· Worksheets	· Independent reading
· Copying spelling words	· Partner reading
· Looking up definitions for spelling words	· Discussion groups/literature circles
· Unrelated computer games	· Responses to reading (based on extending and deepening the reading experience)
· Arts and crafts	· Inquiry projects and research based on interest
· Nonsense word practice	· Demonstration and reflection of strategy use in context of independent reading

Figure 1.2 Purposeful learning experiences

We know it's not as simple as it looks. The goal of this book is to make transparent how we developed independence with emerging decoders so they could participate in the PLEs without teacher support. We relied on five research-based principles to assist us in that process.

● Five Research-Based Principles for Fostering Independence in Literacy

Each research-based principle is centered around a successful component of early literacy instruction as documented by studies in the field of literacy. In addition to the formalized research literature, each principle is one we have found to be useful in our journey as primary teachers when fostering independence with PLEs. Each chapter will offer teaching moves based on these research-based principles.

DEVELOP A NURTURING ENVIRONMENT

The community of the classroom extends beyond rules and routines. As Vygotsky (1978) and Wells (1999) note, learning is a socially situated practice. Young children develop a sense of themselves and a reader identity within the context of the class-room community. We want students to develop a positive identity and know that we celebrate taking risks to stretch thinking and become better readers. Reading development is always a work in progress. When this is a common understanding in the community, students can identify goals and celebrate their successes without fear of embarrassment.

Students successfully take risks with language and literacy in an inquiry-based community. Their eagerness to be part of the primary-aged classroom community increases motivation, engagement, and independent literacy development (Guccione 2010). Additionally, Krashen (1987) reports that as English learners begin to feel safe in a classroom, they lower their "affective filter." Reducing anxiety or emotions allows students to understand and retain more information than they would in a less-supportive classroom environment. The research supports the importance of developing a nurturing environment, and we couldn't agree more. Sometimes young children become competitive when there is a focus on skills, Accelerated Reader scores, or text levels. This can lead to embarrassment and resistance to reading. We take a meaning-based approach to supporting development by providing opportunities for choice in text selection (without leveling), discussion about texts of interest, individual goal setting and strategy documentation, and time for students to share their reading progress and experiences.

APPRECIATE CHOICE

We all appreciate choice. We found choice to be the most essential component of successfully fostering independence. We provide students with choices for texts, topics, strategy use, responses, inquiry projects, and discussion groups. We understand the importance of emerging readers having time to read texts at their independent levels, and we help students make sure to select at least a couple of books each week that fit into that category. However, this does not necessarily correspond with a specific level. Halladay (2008, 2012) found many students can read above their reading level when the book is on a topic of interest. Additionally, Lindsey reported findings of English learners demonstrating higher motivation and engagement when given choice for topic, texts, and response opportunities (Guccione 2010).

In our first-grade experiences together, we were surprised at students' eagerness and natural tendency toward effective use of strategies when given the choice of when and where to use them with texts of interest. Likewise, as students became more independent, the text selections, response choices, and inquiry projects became more sophisticated. Choice leads to motivation and engagement, which leads to greater development and independence, even for our youngest readers.

OFFER SUPPORTED INDEPENDENT READING TIME

Many researchers have documented the benefits of the use of supported independent reading for developing fluency and comprehension in reading (Reis et al. 2008; Reutzel, Fawson, and Smith 2008). Studies have shown the number of minutes students spend reading at school is associated with gains in reading achievement and that teachers are influential in determining how much time students spend at school reading (Taylor, Frye, and Maruyama 1990).

Reading is like learning to play tennis. Yes, you need instruction and support, but you have to play to get better. You will never develop an amazing slice serve by listening to an expert talk about it all day. The more time you spend practicing with support (coaching), the better you get. We believe this is true with reading and "approximated reading." Students who use approximated reading are in the natural developmental process of moving toward conventional reading. We believe in giving them time to practice. Although there is some resistance to giving extended periods of time for independent reading when students are not yet conventionally decoding text, we agree with Kathy Collins and Matt Glover (2015) when they say, "In the rush toward even higher reading levels in the early years, we may fail to value the strategy use and high-level thinking children do before they are reading conventionally" (4). So, the moral of this principle is support them, and regardless of their reading level, let them read!

CREATE OPPORTUNITIES FOR TALK AND INTERACTION

Research has shown discussion and dialogic teaching support comprehension (Nystrand 2006; Wells 1999), so we created multiple opportunities for talk and interaction related to reading. To do this, we had to foster independence in ways of responding and talking about texts. We drew on Sipe's (2007) work that documented the various types of responses young children might have, including analytical, intertextual, personal, transparent, and performative responses. Students develop their response repertoires so they can participate in meaningful discussions with peers.

Discussion groups engage students in higher-level thinking and help them clarify understanding, apply comprehension strategies, and communicate knowledge together (Kelley and Clausen-Grace 2013; Roche 2015). Discussion groups also allow teachers and students the opportunity to hear and value all children's voices (Moses, Ogden, and Kelly 2015). However, students must develop confidence, competence, and collaborative independence to participate in meaningful ways in the primary grades. We address the detail of this idea in greater depth in Chapters 6 and 7, but the basis of this principle is supporting students to participate in meaningful talk about text without the teacher.

USE ASSESSMENT TO GUIDE INSTRUCTION

Assessment plays an essential role in informing instruction. Assessment that gives teachers immediate feedback on instructional needs improves the quality of classroom teaching (Allington and Cunningham 2002). Because of this, we recommend teachers ask themselves, "What do I want to know? Why do I want to know it? How can I best discover it?" (Opitz and Guccione 2009). This gives teachers an opportunity to gather valuable assessment data to make purposeful instructional choices. We take into consideration all of the required assessments from the district, but we also believe that assessment "is a social practice that involves noticing, representing, and responding to children's literate behaviors, rendering them meaningful for particular purposes and audiences" (Johnston and Costello 2005, 258).

This idea guides our framework for fostering independence with young readers. Building on this notion of assessment, we get a deeper understanding of our students' literacy competencies by observing students, examining student responses, engaging with children during discussions, and conferring and coaching on a regular basis. We begin all of our instruction with observing children because they don't need support in areas where they are already demonstrating meaningful independence. We recommend using assessments that provide immediate instructional feedback to guide you through the process of supporting independent readers.

• What to Expect in This Book

We provide lesson plans, assessment tools, student samples, and classroom vignettes to make transparent the "how-to" part of creating independent readers. It takes time, and we take you through our progression and process of enhancing independent learning experiences for young children. Our student-centered model for fostering independence includes the following components:

- preassessing
- teaching
- scaffolding
- monitoring and refining
- extending
- assessing

In Chapter 2, we identify essential components for environments and scheduling that foster independence and discuss how they change and evolve over the course of the year based on the students' needs. We include classroom layouts and photographs of primary classrooms.

In Chapter 3, we focus on creating classroom routines to support independence. We share two essential routines that allow students to move through the literacy period without teacher support or redirection: book shopping and library management, and building and maintaining stamina. We utilize our student-centered model to share the six stages of facilitating independent routines.

Chapter 4 addresses the importance of introducing strategies that support independent reading with emergent readers. To be independent, students must have strategies to support their reading. We share the progression of facilitating independence with two types of strategies: fix-up strategies and comprehension strategies. We include multiple assessments including note-taking guides and observational checklists.

In Chapter 5, we introduce authentic and meaningful response opportunities that support and deepen independent reading experiences. We share the six stages of facilitating independence with reading response journals and self-selected inquiry projects. This chapter includes student samples and rubrics.

Chapter 6 addresses partner experiences where students are able to collaborate without the direct support of the teacher. We identify two types of partner reading opportunities: coaching and talking. As we share the process of introducing and extending these experiences, we include anchor charts, bookmarks, and assessment tools (note-taking guides and observational checklists).

In Chapter 7, we discuss small-group collaborative independence. We share the process of supporting student-led, small-group reading opportunities for primary students. These experiences include the introduction, development, refinement, and assessment of student-directed literature discussion groups and performance groups.

2 · Environment and Schedules that Foster Independence

"Meet the teacher" night has finally arrived, and Aubri enters the classroom holding her mother's hand. Her wide eyes carefully dart around the room as she takes it all in. She appears nervous, but intrigued. She comes to a halt as she approaches the fiction section of our library and quietly whispers, "Look at all the books!" She flips through a basket, pulls out a book, sits on our pink couch, and begins to read. She smiles up at her mother with great ease, and at that moment, we know Aubri feels at home. We hope all our children feel welcomed and invited to learn in our shared space. It is not Mrs. Ogden's classroom. It is our classroom, a place where we will learn and grow together.

🐜 🐜 🐜

Creating an inviting space that supports students' independence does not happen overnight. Our classroom and philosophical thinking have evolved over the years. In doing so, we traded desks for community tables. We said good-bye to our clunky teacher desk and hello to cozy reading spots. We expanded our library until it became the central hub for learning. We accumulated more pillows, beanbags, and reading buddies. We brightened the room with lamps. We took down generic posters, leaving space for student work and co-created anchor charts. We took the supplies out of the cupboards, giving children access to what they needed, but most importantly we created a student-centered environment—a space where children like Aubri feel at home.

• Why Environment and Schedules Matter

Lella Gandini (2012), a renowned Reggio Emilia advocate and researcher, said, "A visitor to any institution for young children tends to size up the messages that the space gives about the quality of care and about the educational choices that form the basis of the program" (318). Reggio-inspired educators refer to the environment as the "third teacher." A thoughtful environment can shape the way children participate, collaborate, and learn. Purposeful environmental design helps nurture and foster independence with

12

young children. The environment is an evolving system. "More than the physical space, it includes the way time is structured and the roles we are expected to play" (Gandini 2012, 332). We completely agree with this philosophy. We carefully crafted, coordinated, and adjusted our physical space and schedule to support students' independence.

• Essential Components of Classroom Space

The two most crucial factors in designing classroom spaces are purpose and access. These are important considerations for the broader design of the entire classroom, but also of the specifically designated spaces like the library or meeting space. Figure 2.1 gives you a sense of our general classroom layout last year (it often changes). The spaces are both specific and flexible. Students know what they are supposed to be doing in each space, but certain spaces can serve various purposes. Everything that students might need to use during the literacy block can be accessed without teacher support.

Supplies like crayons, glue, scissors, pencils, erasers, and so on are in shared community baskets on each table. Sticky notes are available on cabinet doors (can be seen in Figure 2.2; see Chapter 4 for more information and pictures). Spaces are designated for additional resources, with white-boards, tissues, folders, additional paper, clipboards, the book hospital box, extra crayons, different types of glue, and pillows/beanbags/comfy seating tools. The cabinet on the right in Figure 2.2 has individual cubbies for each student, where they receive notes from us and submit work. Giving students access to everything they need prevents time off-task and interruptions while we are conferring or meeting with small groups. Designated space provides purpose; the only thing students do in the resources space is quickly grab what they need and return to their work (independent reading, responding, partner reading, inquiry projects, discussion groups, and so on). Every part of our environment has a clear purpose and is easily accessible.

Figure 2.1 Classroom layout

Figure 2.2 Resource area where students can easily access comfortable seating options, clipboards, and extra supplies

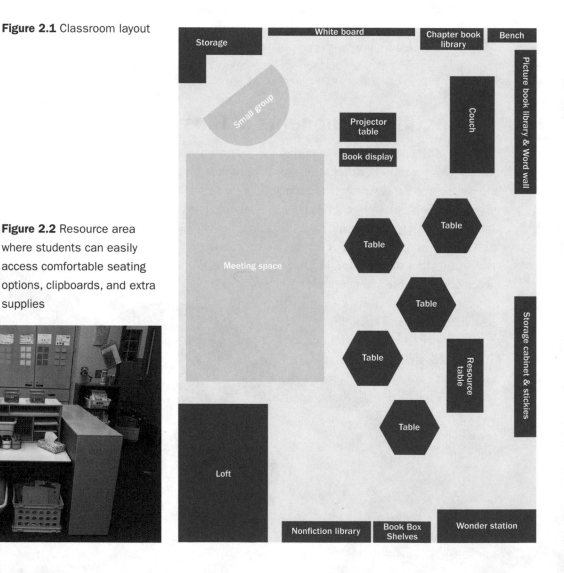

MEETING SPACE

The meeting space brings students together for minilessons and whole-class discussions. In previous years, we used a large carpet that had colored squares to designate this space, but we had too many students to fit on the squares. The meeting space is distinct but flexible; students also use this space for independent and partner reading as seen in Figure 2.3. Figure 2.4 shows a rocking chair in front of the meeting space for the teacher to sit in during minilessons, and students know the collaborative anchor charts will be created on the chart paper and easel next to the chair, as seen in Figure 2.5. The featured focus lesson of the day or week is displayed on the wall next to the easel. Sometimes the anchor charts require student contribution throughout the week. Figure 2.6 shows Valentina adding her thinking to our narrative elements anchor chart. There are no distractions in this space. Our time here is brief, so students don't need access to anything. They only need to bring their bodies (and books during discussion group). Figure 2.7 shows how we utilize the space during discussion groups.

Figure 2.3 Isha, Sophia, Alexis, Ava, and Mason find comfortable spaces during independent reading.

Figure 2.4 The view students see when they walk in the door. The open space is used for lessons, meetings, discussion groups, and independent and partner reading.

Figure 2.5 Meridith teaches a minilesson on partner reading and talk in the meeting space.

Figure 2.6 Valentina adds to the interactive chart some important learning she documented earlier, during independent reading.

Figure 2.7 The whole class comes together in a circle after independent reading. Students bring their books and are prepared to share and discuss their best thinking with peers.

SMALL-GROUP SPACE

We use the kidney bean table behind the carpet space for small-group instruction (Figure 2.4). Students can sit wherever they choose. We often suggest they sit in a circle around the table so they can all make eye contact, particularly during discussion groups. Students bring their book boxes and a pencil. With guided reading groups or when introducing a new literature discussion group, we provide the books. However, in strategy groups, we briefly introduce a strategy students all need, model it, ask them to try it with a book they have for independent reading, and coach as needed (Serravallo 2010). Students know the purpose is short, focused instruction with opportunities to apply reading strategies with coaching and support or to discuss books and thinking with peers.

There are also times when we are conferring and not pulling small groups. When conferring, we go to wherever students are reading and working, as seen in Figure 2.8. This leaves the small-group space open for students to read and work independently or with partners. They also love to bring a pillow or beanbag behind the table and nestle into the corner for some secluded reading.

TEACHER'S SPACE

We don't have a teacher's desk. This is purposeful. Teacher's desks take up space and create a sense of power. Teachers' desks often become a space that is not part of the community or is off-limits to students. Our teacher "stuff" (binders, assessments, grade books, resources, and so on) is stored in the file cabinets, organizers, and bookshelves behind our small-group space as seen in Figure 2.4. We also have a community desk where we put the computer and/or doc camera when we need to project things.

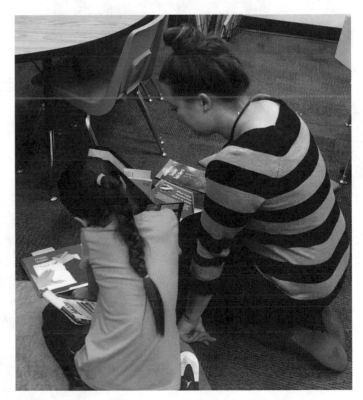

Figure 2.8 Meridith joins Mia on her comfy pillow for a short conference about text selection and strategy use.

READING SPACE

Readers read almost everywhere in our room. We talk more specifically about the guidelines for this in Chapter 3. We try to create comfortable spaces for all readers. Some like to kneel and read at a short table. Others enjoy lying on beanbags, the couch, or loft spaces. Still others just want to sit in their seat at a table. These are all viable options during independent and partner reading. We specifically established expectations for how many could be on the couch or loft at one time, but other than that, students can read wherever they want. Figures 2.9 and 2.10 are images of the most popular reading spots: the couch, bench, and loft.

Figure 2.9 The close proximity to the library makes the couch an even more inviting space.

Figure 2.10 The loft (top and bottom) offers cozy reading spaces with pillows, soft lighting, and displays of favorite book covers.

Students are more productive and independent when they are in comfortable spaces. Figures 2.11, 2.12, 2.13, 2.14, and 2.15 show what this looks like in action.

Figure 2.11 Some students don't prefer beanbags or the couch. Leo is his happiest when he is reading informational text in the laundry basket.

Figure 2.12 William and Cameron spend independent reading time in comfortable reading positions on the top of the loft.

Figure 2.13 William and Christian are partner reading under the loft. Christian stops to ask a clarifying question about the page William just read aloud.

Figure 2.14 Emily finished reading a book that inspired her to write. She is authoring a reading response from the couch.

Figure 2.15 Ava and Emily love to be close, even when reading independently. Ava silently reads a book while Emily builds fluency by rereading the weekly poem. Valentina likes a little more space and reads a book nearby on the beanbag.

LIBRARY

The library is the heart of reading independence. This is where students come to browse, return, recommend, and pick out new books each week (we discuss this in detail in Chapter 3). Many teachers level their library, but we organize ours by author, genre, theme, and so on. We have sections of the library around the room. The largest portion of the library seen in Figure 2.9 has baskets of fiction picture books that are easily accessible for students to flip through, pull out, and look at the covers. Other library areas include chapter books and nonfiction baskets. All books have a sticker on the back with a number that corresponds with the book box where it belongs (this number is listed under the category title on the box). The book sets stacked on top of the library are used for discussion groups, so we keep those books back and have a "reveal" for each text during discussion group selection. Students get excited about the mystery and special access for these texts.

We realize we have an extensive library. We are regularly asked, "How did you get so many books?" The truth is that we have been collecting them for years, and most of them were purchased out of our own pocket or through Scholastic book order points. We have also written grants and used Donors Choose. The books and our library are the most valuable tools we have at our disposal for engaging young readers. Students need choice, quality books, a lot of time to read, and a large selection of books. Students store their books, poems, and reading response journals in small boxes that are kept on an easily accessible bookshelf, as seen in Figure 2.16.

Figure 2.16 Students need to be able to easily identify and access their book boxes. Low bookshelves like this one work well.

WALL SPACE

The wall space helps define areas and provides support for readers. Anchor charts around the classroom support the use of recently introduced strategies (we give extensive examples of this in Chapter 4). The wall display in Figure 2.17 was created by the students. As they learn new strategies, they add them to our wall as a point of reference. A high-frequency word wall can be seen above the library shelves in Figure 2.9. Another interactive and defining wall display is our wonder wall. Based on Heard and McDonough's (2009) *A Place for Wonder*, we created a wonder station where students observe and wonder about things. The current wonder station (Figure 2.18) includes various items to observe and wonder about: hermit crabs, feathers, bones, rocks (some things provided by the teacher and others by the students). Students can write their new wonderings and add it to the wonder wall.

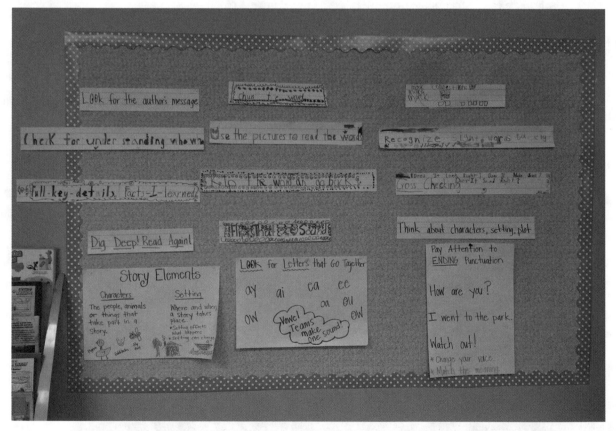

Figure 2.17 Students take ownership of strategies that help them become better readers. This wall includes their documentation (writing and images) of helpful reading strategies as a reference for the class.

Figure 2.18 The wonder station is used to ask questions, think, and observe. Students can add their thinking to the wonder wall.

• Our Schedule

The logistics of scheduling and fitting everything in sometimes feels overwhelming. We had a ninety-minute reading block and a lot of freedom to make professional decisions about our instruction. This is not the case for everyone, so we will offer scheduling alternatives. We did not have an aide in the classroom, and we usually have twenty-seven or more students each year. Even if we wanted, we couldn't divide the class into three small groups with daily rotations because of our class size. We greatly value conferring, needs-based small groups, and strategy groups. We do not have a set rotation; instead, we pull groups based on an assessment (formal and informal) of their needs. Figure 2.19 is a sample schedule. It was flexible and changed throughout the year, but will show you how we scheduled our reading block.

Our students struggled with independence at the beginning of the year and could not be independently productive for long periods. Knowing this, we broke up independent stretches with whole-class discussion circles, check-ins, and additional minilessons. The schedule shows two rows for some blocks of time. In these cases, the top row designates conferring or small-group work, and the bottom row (in italics) denotes what the rest of the students did during those times. The rest of the book focuses on how to foster meaningful independence during the independent and partner reading work periods.

	Monday	Tuesday	Wednesday	Thursday	Friday
10–15 minutes	Minilesson	Minilesson	Minilesson	Minilesson	Book share Literature response Book shopping
20 minutes	Conferring, guided reading, or needs-based strategy groups	Conferring, guided reading, or needs-based strategy groups	Conferring, guided reading, or needs-based strategy groups	Conferring, guided reading, or needs-based strategy groups	
	Independent reading work	*Independent reading work*	*Independent reading work*	*Independent reading work*	
5–10 minutes	Whole-class discussion circle and check-in	Whole-class discussion circle and check-in	Whole-class discussion circle and check-in	Whole-class discussion circle and check-in	Whole-class discussion circle and check-in
20 minutes	Conferring, guided reading, or needs-based strategy groups	Conferring, guided reading, or needs-based strategy groups	Conferring, guided reading, or needs-based strategy groups	Conferring, guided reading, or needs-based strategy groups	Conferring, guided reading, or needs-based strategy groups
	Partner reading work	*Partner reading work*	*Partner reading work*	*Partner reading work*	*Partner reading work*
10–15 minutes	Minilesson	Minilesson	Minilesson	Minilesson	Minilesson
20 minutes	Conferring, guided reading, or needs-based strategy groups	Conferring, guided reading, or needs-based strategy groups	Conferring, guided reading, or needs-based strategy groups	Conferring, guided reading, or needs-based strategy groups	Conferring, guided reading, or needs-based strategy groups
	Partner reading work	*Partner reading work*	*Partner reading work*	*Partner reading work*	*Partner reading work*
5 minutes	Wrap-up and share	Wrap-up and share	Wrap-up and share	Wrap-up and share	Wrap-up and share

Figure 2.19 Sample Schedule

• Alternative Schedules

Many teachers have less freedom when it comes to scheduling small-group instruction. Lindsey has worked with many schools to facilitate meaningful independence within various contexts. The scheduling and logistics always seem to be an initial challenge. Many schools require a specific small-group rotation. Typically, the students who need the most support receive daily targeted small-group instruction. The schedule found in Figure 2.20 was used in a large first-grade classroom (twenty-eight students with no paraprofessional support). That school required the neediest students (Group 1) receive small-group instruction five days a week and preferred that the other groups were seen three to four times a week.

This schedule was set up similar to ours with segments divided into what the teacher was doing and what the students were doing. There are a couple of differences. The students were placed in groups in ascending order based on their benchmark assessment instructional levels. We tried to balance time as much as possible with Groups 2 and 3. Group 4 was only scheduled to meet twice a week, but the teacher typically met with those students once or twice a week during the ten- to fifteen-minute conference or needs-based strategy group time following the minilesson.

This schedule would be much simpler and easy to modify if the class only had three groups because they would fit easily into the daily rotation. If you have a smaller primary class, this is a possibility. However, we think it is important to show how we made it work, even in challenging settings.

	Monday	Tuesday	Wednesday	Thursday	Friday
10–12 minutes	Minilesson	Minilesson	Minilesson	Minilesson	Book share Literature response Book shopping
10–15 minutes	Conferring, needs-based strategy groups, or discussion group prep	Conferring or needs-based strategy groups	Conferring or needs-based strategy groups	Conferring or needs-based strategy groups	
	Independent reading work	*Independent reading work*	*Independent reading work*	*Independent reading work*	
20 minutes	Small Group 1: guided reading or strategy groups	Small Group 1: guided reading or strategy groups	Small Group 1: guided reading or strategy groups	Small Group 1: guided reading or strategy groups	Small Group 1: guided reading or strategy groups
	Independent reading work	*Independent reading work*	*Independent reading work*	*Independent reading work*	*Independent reading work*
5–7 minutes	Whole-class discussion circle and check-in	Whole-class discussion circle and check-in	Whole-class discussion circle and check-in	Whole-class discussion circle and check-in	Whole-class discussion circle and check-in
20 minutes	Small Group 2: guided reading or strategy groups	Small Group 2: guided reading or strategy groups	Small Group 3: guided reading or strategy groups	Small Group 2: guided reading or strategy groups	Small Group 3: guided reading or strategy groups
	Partner reading work	*Partner reading work*	*Partner reading work*	*Partner reading work*	*Partner reading work*
15 minutes	Small Group 3: guided reading or strategy groups	Small Group 4: guided reading or strategy groups	Small Group 2: guided reading or strategy groups	Small Group 3: guided reading or strategy groups	Small Group 4: guided reading or strategy groups
	Partner reading work	*Partner reading work*	*Partner reading work*	*Partner reading work*	*Partner reading work*
2–5 minutes	Wrap-up and share	Wrap-up and share	Wrap-up and share	Wrap-up and share	Wrap-up and share

Figure 2.20 Alternative Schedule

3 · Routines that Foster Independence

It's Friday morning, and students are shopping for new books. The quiet hum slowly turns into a louder buzz as students collaborate in their quest for fresh titles. They scurry from basket to basket with great intent, stopping to help a friend, make a recommendation, even trade books. In the midst of all the busyness, Landon calls out, "Class, class." The students stop in their tracks and respond, "Yes, yes." He asks, "Does anyone have The Three Ninja Pigs?" *Dax tells him it's probably with the other folktales, and Farah and Allisson head* over to initiate the search.

Across the room, Loraina eagerly waves Olivia over, asking whether she still has the pigeon book. Olivia lets her down easy: "I already gave it to Owen, but maybe next week." Mia and Wyatt crouch over the basket containing space-related books, opening each one, looking for more information about Jupiter. Near the beginning chapter books, Sarah offers her Frog and Toad *book to some nearby shoppers. Mia gasps and takes the book with a smile.*

Students gradually settle into cozy independent reading spots, oblivious to the sound of feet still moving about the classroom shopping for books. Ramone is sitting in the middle of the library, lost in a good book, paying no attention to the shoppers around him. Allisson is still thoughtfully browsing the library, searching for the perfect book. Alex quietly shares his new titles with his cousin Leo. The classroom brims with the quiet hum of little readers.

Friday mornings are the best. The students are eager to shop for new books, but more importantly, they share their passion with one another. It is a social time, a time to build relationships around books and learn together. We support these readers by responding to their questions: "You know that book you read last week, about the bear and the hat, do we have any more books by that author?" "Where can I find Grouchy Ladybug?" *Diego says, "I read all the dinosaur books and all the shark books, but I just have to know more about megalodons and we are out of books. Can we get a book on just megalodons?" How can you say no to a child who wants to read more and with such great intention? We immediately order Diego's book about megalodons. We are resources for our students, literary docents with a shared passion for reading who help these children see the beauty in literature. Giving children time to explore and choose their own books creates readers who choose to read, which is exactly what we want.*

🐛 🐛 🐛

By May, students were self-sufficient, participating in routines that required little or no support from us. Their collaborative interactions supported discussing, recommending, sharing, and finding texts independently. This was not the case at the beginning of the year. Students come to school with different experiences and expectations for how to select and engage with books. In this chapter, we focus on being explicit about creating, maintaining, and extending classroom routines to support independence throughout the year.

Many primary teachers want students to be independent, but worry that independent reading and student-centered approaches do not work in the primary grades because of students' independent decoding abilities. They report that students struggle to select books that are of high interest and appropriate readability levels. Additionally, students experience behavior and attention span challenges during independent reading opportunities. We regularly hear, "They can't read yet, so they are just wasting time and getting in trouble" and "I tried it, but they could only do it for a few minutes.

It seems like I have to supervise them or they will just look at the books and don't know what to do." These are valid concerns, but they can be overcome. Routines for managing book selection and building reading stamina need to be established at the beginning of the year and must be revisited and extended.

We utilized our student-centered model to help students develop two essential routines that foster independence: book shopping, and building and maintaining independent reading stamina.

● Supporting Research: Why Is It Important? Does It Really Work?

The amount of time students spend reading in school is associated with gains in reading achievement, and this holds true for beginning readers, struggling readers, and students reading in a second language. Independent reading also fosters positive attitudes toward reading, especially in the primary grades (Yoon 2002). Researchers have validated the efficacy of scaffolded and supported independent reading for developing fluency and comprehension in reading (Reis et al. 2008; Reutzel, Fawson, and Smith 2008). Scaffolded silent reading includes instruction in selecting "good-fit" books and teacher conferences with four to five students per day.

Action research reports and qualitative descriptions of exemplary literacy teaching reveal multiple modifications that successful teachers have made to silent reading to enhance engagement and achievement. In independent reading, teachers provide direct instruction, guidance, and suggestions on text selections as children learn to select books that meet their interests and are within or just above their reading levels (Sanden 2014; Sanden 2012; Trudel 2007). Additional research indicates children can learn to select books appropriate to their reading level (Wutz and Wedwick 2005). Other strategies teachers have employed to support independent reading include offering high-interest books (Kelley and Clausen-Grace 2009); adding read-alouds to model reading engagement, stamina, and reading behaviors such as not disturbing others and staying in one spot (Sanden 2014); and monitoring these behaviors among students (Trudel 2007).

Finally, many teachers now relinquish the expectation that independent reading be silent reading, especially in early grades. It is particularly necessary for primary teachers to acknowledge the developmental process that students work through as they progress toward silent reading and permit the whisper reading or subvocalizing that beginning readers often do (Wright, Sherman, and Jones 2004). In fact, students up to sixth grade may benefit in comprehension when they read aloud. This understanding of the value of independent reading and the need to provide instructional supports for it led to our yearlong investigation of fostering students' independence with scaffolded independent reading.

Book Shopping

Managing the classroom library requires a delicate balance between organization, choice, behavior, and matching children with appropriate texts. In Meridith's classroom, students shopped for books every Friday, right before they began reading independently. We tried having different groups of students shop on different days, as well as letting students shop whenever they wanted to, but we found that shopping as a class created opportunities for collaboration, discussion, and recommendation and took less time. Once students selected their books, they found a spot and began reading.

Classroom libraries can be organized in many ways—by genre, series, or some other category (see Chapter 2). Sharon Taberski (2000) suggests having bins of unleveled books from which students choose their independent reading selections and bins of books by level for when they need practice with something "just right." Other teachers label their books using the Fountas and Pinnell A through Z gradient.

Although we agree with the experts (Allington 2009; Hiebert and Fisher 2012) that students need to spend time with independent-level text (typically 97–100 percent accuracy), we are also aware that an "assessed" reading level doesn't always correspond with a student's level of comprehension (Halladay 2012). Therefore, we spent a great deal of time supporting independent text selection that included texts that supported decoding development, fostered comprehension and thinking, and piqued students' interest in reading.

PREASSESSING

1. Ask students to select books for independent reading.
2. Observe them as they do so.
3. Observe independent reading.
4. Have them discuss their book-shopping and reading experience.

We first identified student needs related to book shopping. Matching our students with books they would enjoy was at the top of our list of ways to support them. Students completed an "interest inventory" at the beginning of the year. This inventory gave us background knowledge about texts that might appeal to different students.

Most of the students in our classroom had not yet had opportunities to self-select texts or spend extended amounts of time reading independently. We asked students to explore the library and select books to read. We watched students quickly select books without taking much time to browse. We noticed multiple areas that needed support, but the most pressing issue was that the majority of students selected books that were much too difficult to decode independently. We did not intervene, but instead watched how they engaged with the text. We called everyone together and asked the students to talk about whether they liked one of the books they selected and why it was or wasn't a good choice. We pointed out Shaun's comment—"This book is a good fit for me because I enjoyed myself and I could read most of the words"—as a model. Then, we began planning a minilesson to support the identification and selection of independent-level texts in addition to high-interest texts.

TEACHING

1. Ask students to discuss what constitutes a good book selection for their independent reading.
2. Expand on students' thinking to introduce good-fit (aka just-right, Goldilocks, independent-level) books.
3. Provide an anchor chart with good-fit criteria.
4. Guide a student as she models applying the criteria.
5. Have students turn and talk about the process for finding a good-fit book.
6. Familiarize students with the classroom library.
7. With student input, generate a list of appropriate book-shopping behavior.

Based on our observations, identified needs, and discussion of book selection, we created a minilesson to introduce how to select and find appropriate books and expectations for behavior during book shopping. We began by asking what sort of book was appropriate for independent reading and got responses like "not too hard" and "not a baby book." We told the students they were correct—like Goldilocks, they should look for books that were "just right." We created a good-fit anchor chart (see Figure 3.1), telling students that a book that meets at least two of these criteria could be considered a good fit.

Next, we showed them an example of a textbook, a board book of the alphabet, and *Go, Dog. Go!* We asked a student to come up and answer the questions to see if he could find a book that worked for at least two of the guidelines (our criteria for a good fit). Evan volunteered and answered no to all of the guidelines for the textbook, no to all but one ("You can read most of the words") for the ABC book; and yes to all of them for *Go, Dog. Go!* The students then turned and talked about what questions they were going to ask themselves during their next shopping opportunity to determine if the book was a good fit. To find these good-fit or just-right books, the students needed to become familiar with the classroom library. We gave them a brief tour of the various tubs and genres/categories, pointing out that the stickers on the back of the books had a number that corresponded with a number on the book tub it was stored in.

Figure 3.1 "Good-Fit Books" anchor chart

They then helped us generate a list of appropriate shopping behaviors (this will vary with grade level, library organization, and general behavior guidelines). Our initial list included taking turns, putting a book back in the correct tub if you decide not to take it, being quiet, making room for other students to look at books, not taking all the books in a series (Mo Willems was very popular and students felt it wouldn't be fair for one student to take all of them at once). Figure 3.2 is the resulting anchor chart of what book shopping should look like, sound like, and feel like.

Figure 3.2 This "Book Shopping" anchor chart was created using students' reflection on what book shopping should look like, sound like, and feel like.

SCAFFOLDING

1. Select two books based on students' reading levels and place them in their book box.
2. Place the poem of the week or other familiar text in students' book box.
3. Ask students to shop for four just-right books.

4. Confer with students as they select books.

5. Keep an observational checklist about book selections.

6. Ask students to evaluate their book selections with a partner.

7. Debrief with students about their book selections: encourage students to exchange books that are too difficult, but allow them to keep two high-interest/hard-to-read books. Provide additional instruction/strategies/anchor charts as needed.

8. Highlight areas and book tubs that might have books of high interest and easy readability.

9. Provide specific feedback and suggestions as needed while students book shop a second time.

Peek into Our Classroom

We had already placed two good-fit books in each student's independent reading book box, so they had to choose four on their own (we began the year with six books each week and eventually increased that number to ten). We also included a copy of the poem of the week, which students read together during every morning message. Therefore, we knew they had at least three texts they could independently decode, but we were excited to see their book selections for the week.

While students were selecting their books, we conferred with individuals, easing them toward appropriate choices and noting their selections on a checklist that included the designations *independent, instructional, frustration,* and *frustration and high interest* (see the example in Figure 3.3; a blank template is in the appendices). Not surprisingly, early in the year, even with teacher prompting, most first graders selected books that were of high interest but much too dif-

Difficulty-Level Checklist   8/17/15

Name	Independent	Instructional	Frustration	Frustration & High Interest
Aiden	2		3	1
Alexis		2		4
Ava	4	1		1
Barrett	2	1		3
Cameron	2	1	1	2
Chris	1	2	1	2
Christian	4	2		
Emily	1	2		3
Ethan	1	3		2
Evan	1	4	-	1
Isha	3	2		1
James (Jace)	1	3		2
James C.	3	3		
Jordan	2	2		2
Julia	2	3		1
Justin	1	2		3
Mason N.	2	1	1	2
Mason W.	1	3		2
Paul		2	2	2
Shaun	3	2		1
Sophia	3	3		
Valentina	4	2		
Will C.	2	1		3
Will L.	2	2		2

Figure 3.3 Difficulty-Level Checklist

ficult to decode independently (more on the actual reading of books in the next section).

When they were finished shopping, we asked them to share their selections with a partner and talk about whether or not they thought the books were a good fit. Many students said they had selected books that were probably too difficult, but they also explained that they were interested in the book.

We asked a few students who had made great choices to share their selections. We allowed students to keep two high-interest/

Figure 3.4 "Just Right" anchor chart

hard-to-read books but the other two needed to be exchanged for good-fit/just-right books. We revisited the idea of text difficulty and created an additional anchor chart that lists strategies for deciding whether a book was too easy or too hard (Figure 3.4). We asked students to talk with their partner about books they would keep and books they would exchange. Then, we pointed out areas of the library with books that might be easy and fun to read, reminding students that they would be ready to choose from the chapter book tubs later in the year. During this second round of shopping, we provided more specific feedback and suggestions for students who needed additional support. Students checked in with us after shopping so we could take a look at their selections. This type of feedback and interaction occurred during the first few shopping attempts.

MONITORING AND REFINING

1. After providing book-shopping support for three or four weeks, release full responsibility to your students: let them select all six books.

2. Continue to monitor their selections through observation and the checklist.

3. Assemble needs-based small groups and/or confer with students to support appropriate book selections.

4. Increase the number of books selected during book shopping.

Peek into Our Classroom

The next two stages (maintaining and deepening independence) are the most difficult parts of fostering independence among young readers. We observed students, provided instruction on book shopping based on the identified needs, and supported and scaffolded successful book selection. This initial part of instruction comes intuitively, and we always do it at the beginning of the year, but maintaining and deepening students' independence with appropriate book selections over the course of the academic year is challenging because it is always changing. We often think that because we taught them how to do it and saw they could do it, we can move on to other instructional needs. However, we found great success with our shopping and independent reading time because we continued to monitor and support from a distance.

During the fourth week of book shopping, we reminded students of the good-fit guidelines but no longer provided support or guidance. We also stopped placing two preselected texts in children's book boxes. We did, however, continue to keep a checklist of the books students chose and noticed a number of trends:

- A small group of students always chose three or four books at their frustration level.
- Some students kept the same books for several weeks.
- Some students read a narrow variety of texts (only Eric Carle or only nonfiction, for example).

Because the majority of students were picking appropriate books, we assembled needs-based small groups to confer with students about their selections and revisit the criteria. As the semester progressed, we increased the number of self-selected books to ten.

DEEPENING

1. Encourage students to talk and interact while they are shopping for books.
2. Create opportunities to collaborate and make recommendations by setting up a formal way to get the attention of the class and ask for help.
3. Incorporate book talks and sharing sessions.
4. Gradually increase the number of books selected.

Peek into Our Classroom

By the second semester, all students could shop for books independently. We asked ourselves, "How can we deepen their book-shopping experiences and extend their independence with selecting books?"

One day late in the semester, we asked Johnathan if he'd selected some good books during shopping. He said, "All but one." Surprised, we asked him what happened and why he had picked a book he did not like. He responded,

> "Well, I don't like Mo Willems, but José [his reading partner] wasn't here yet when we were shopping, and he loves Mo Willems, so I grabbed one before they were all gone."

> "You don't like Mo Willems?"

> "No, I only like nonfiction, but he's José's favorite author."

This got us thinking about the collaborative nature of selecting, recommending, reading, and discussing books with peers. We encouraged students to help one another shop for books, collaborate, and make suggestions. We instituted the practice, borrowed from *Whole Brain Teaching for Challenging Kids* (Biffle 2013), of getting everyone's attention by calling, "Class, class." The rest of the students then responded, "Yes, yes," and looked at the speaker, who then asked for help. For example, Jose asked, "Does anyone have an insect book?" Students showed him the book tub where he might find it, and another student brought him an insect book she had been reading. We also encouraged students to recommend books to other students based on

Figure 3.5 Farah and Aubri excitedly read together after getting two copies of the same book while book shopping together.

what they knew about these students' reading preferences. Figure 3.5 shows partners who shopped together so they could each have a copy of books they selected to read together.

We also incorporated a brief discussion circle after independent reading so students could share the book they were reading and the number of the tub in which it was stored. These peer recommendations sparked new and more diverse interests: students were exposed to new genres, series, and ideas. Figure 3.6 shows students browsing and shopping for possible discussion group readings. Book shopping became

Figure 3.6 We placed new sets of books on the table for students to browse and shop for discussion group options. Aiden, Loraina, Diego, and Leo talk about and explore the books and make selections for upcoming discussion groups.

a social and productive time when students engaged with books and one another in the process of finding new, interesting books for the week. Additionally, we gradually increased the number of independent reading books from six to ten per week.

ASSESSING

Assessment needs to take place throughout the year. Observation informed much of our instruction about selecting books independently. However, we also used some more formal tools to assess students' book-shopping, like the interest inventory and checklist of text difficulty. We also kept track of weekly book selections by scanning each student's choices into his or her "bookshelf" on the Delicious Library app. Additional assessment ideas include reading response journals and rubrics (see Chapter 5).

Considerations in kindergarten and second grade

	Teacher Modifications	Student Expectations
K	· Use images to help students identify types/ genres of books for easy book location. · Provide additional support for text selection. · Provide additional support for a greater length of time. · Increase number of books or allow students to shop more frequently because the books are shorter and often repetitive. · Modify book recommendation format.	· Read short and repetitive texts. · Select high-interest texts. · Navigate the classroom library. · Use oral language to recommend texts to friends.
2	· Decrease the number of texts students get each week (as the text complexity increases). · Allow students to keep books for longer periods. · Introduce more sophisticated options for book recommendations and collaboration.	· Read more complex text like chapter books that can't be completed in one reading. · Use the "five finger rule" to accurately assess and select appropriate texts. · Easily navigate the classroom library. · Collaborate and recommend texts to peers.

At the end of a minilesson on making connections, we remind students that good readers think while they read. We encourage students to look for deeper connections in their books and ask them to be prepared to share these connections when we meet again as a class. They nod, looking at us with eager eyes, knowing we are about to send the first group of children off to get their book box and settle in for independent reading. They all want to be first, not because they will get a better spot, but because independent reading is special and they are a community of readers who value reading well-crafted books.

Book-shopping calendar

	Week 1	Week 2	Week 3	Week 4	Week 5	Week 6	Week 7–Dec.	Jan.	Feb.–June
Interest inventory	X								
Introduce book shopping	X								
Two teacher-selected/four student-selected books, conferring, and feedback	X	X	X						
Difficulty-Level Checklist	X	X	X	X					
Withdrawal of teacher book-shopping support and teacher-selected texts				X	X	X	X		
Needs-based small groups				X	X	X			
Introduce more sophisticated book analysis								X	
Collaborative shopping opportunities							X	X	X
Book recommendations and discussions								X	X

Groups hurry off, grab their book boxes, and find a just-right spot. Within a few minutes, the entire class is settled in. After a quick glance to be sure everyone is on track for success, we are off to confer with individuals.

Our first stop is Allisson, who is rapt by a Kevin Henkes book. Our plan is to talk with her about making good-fit book choices, but we notice the pages of her book are filled with orange sticky notes (our color for connections). When we ask about them, she explains each connection in detail; even though the book is beyond her instructional level, she understands the story and, more importantly, she is thinking while reading. Our conference confirms that she is reading with purpose and internalizing our strategy instruction. We jot down a few notes and walk away with a great feeling.

We make a few more stops, conferring with students about their strategy use, providing additional scaffolds, and encouraging them to make connections while reading. Because the students are reading independently, we are able to move easily from student to student. Our conferring and their reading are purposeful, but none of it would have been possible had we not spent the time building stamina and discussing successful reading habits.

🐾 🐾 🐾

Building and Maintaining Independent Reading Stamina

Independent reading is a critical aspect of effective literacy instruction and an important support for reading development, but many primary teachers struggle with providing scaffolds for emerging decoders. Book shopping and selection positively impact students' participation in independent reading, but some need additional support. Many are not yet decoding printed text independently, but this doesn't mean they are not reading. As Kathy Collins and Matt Glover (2015) note, young readers move through stages of independence that include using the pictures, retelling familiar stories, inferring character's words and feelings, and drawing on content or background knowledge to make meaning. We support these developmental processes of emergent literacy and introduce them as options to our readers to build confidence and facilitate independence.

We tried a variety of approaches to independent reading during the workshop time, ranging from "The Daily Five" (Boushey and Moser 2014) to sustained silent reading to reading response logs. However, these approaches provided few opportunities to deepen students' independent engagement with text at a wide range of reading levels. We often felt we were simply keeping (or attempting to keep) students quiet and busy while we conferred with students individually or worked with small groups. Our goal was to facilitate independence among our emerging readers with meaningful reading opportunities that deepened their engagement with text.

PREASSESSING

1. Ask students to find a place in the room to read to themselves.
2. Observe their behavior as they read.
3. Create observational notes and/or a checklist to document what you notice readers doing.

Observation is one of the best strategies for providing effective, student-driven instruction. A quick look around the room gave us a general idea of what students were doing during independent reading, but as we began jotting observational notes, we noticed the wide range of ways students were engaging (or not) with texts and created a checklist that included each behavior we observed. Figure 3.7 includes an example. A blank template is included in the appendices.

We completed this checklist for the entire class once a week, adding categories as needed. It usually took no more than two minutes to complete and allowed us to document important information we could share with students, parents, and administrators. During this observation, we noticed students needed additional support in ways they could engage with texts and their expectations during independent reading.

Independent Reading Observational Checklist 7/28/15

	Reading aloud	Reading silently	Tracking text	Pointing to pictures	Related talking	Looking at pictures/cover	Getting up	Staring at one page	Playing with book	Playing with other children	Unrelated talking	Seeking adult assistance
LK	\		\									
OW	\											
BL	\	\	\\									
CR							\		\	\		
CW						\		\				
ML				\	\							
NA	\\											ן
BE							\				\	
EL	\		\									

Figure 3.7 First-week literate behavior checklist

TEACHING

1. Ask students to discuss what they do when they read a book by themselves.

2. Build on students' thinking by sharing the four primary ways of reading a book.

3. Create an anchor chart listing these four ways, with supporting images.

4. Using a familiar book, model (with student input) each way of reading.

5. Have students turn and talk about their four options for reading books.

6. With your students, create an anchor chart summarizing why reading independently is important and how to do so successfully.

7. Read the list together or have students read it with a partner before independent reading sessions.

Peek into Our Classroom

Based on the observed needs, we had two goals. Our first goal was to add one more way of reading to the three identified in "The Daily Five" approach (Boushey and Moser 2014). Although we liked the simple, concise options of reading the pictures, reading the words, and retelling the story, focusing on written text and illustrations often overshadows paying attention to design elements (Serafini and Moses 2015).

Therefore, we added the more sophisticated option of drawing on all meaning-making systems (pictures, words, and design elements) simultaneously to support comprehension (see Figure 3.8). We interactively modeled each option using *Pete the Cat*, a familiar book well loved by first graders. We drew attention to design elements like typographical features; the book's size, shape, and orientation; the cover; and the peritextual features such as endpapers and covers, which add to the overall experience of reading picture books. Students immediately began to rely on these multiple cueing systems.

Our second goal was to establish the purpose and expectations of independent reading. With our students, we prepared another anchor chart summarizing why reading independently is important and how to do so successfully (Figure 3.9).

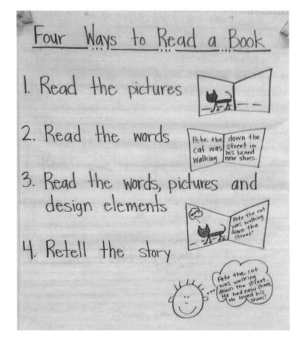

Figure 3.8 "Four Ways to Read a Book" anchor chart

SCAFFOLDING

1. Review expectations for independent reading.

2. Explain that you will be observing and timing how long students can meet these expectations.

3. Help students select reading spots.

4. Observe them while they read, completing a behavior checklist as you do.

5. Call students back together as soon as you see someone not following the guidelines.

6. Ask students to reflect on what went well and why they think you ended the session.

7. Create a chart keeping track of the length of each independent reading session.

8. Set goals with students to increase the time they spend on task during independent reading.

9. Continue to complete the behavior checklist and share what you observe with students.

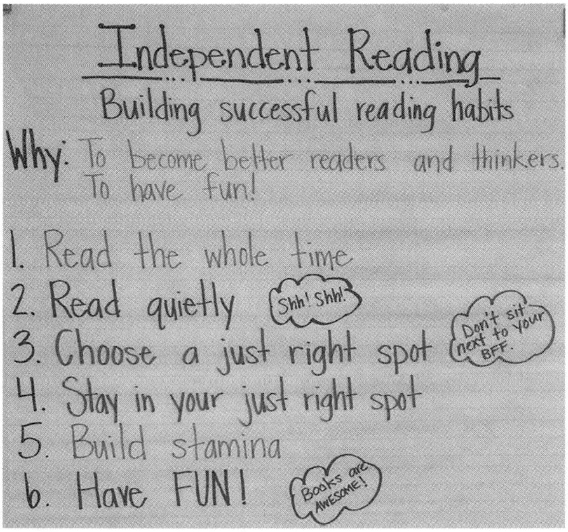

Figure 3.9 The "Independent Reading" anchor chart includes the purpose, procedures, and additional speech bubbles based on students' comments, discussions, and reactions. Adapted from Boushey and Moser (2014).

Peek into Our Classroom

We sent our students off to read independently but told them we would end the session if we noticed anyone not following the guidelines they had just helped us create. We asked them to work hard on building their reading stamina and told them we were going to observe, take notes, and time how long they were able to read to themselves. Students then grabbed their book box and found a good spot in which to read. Once everyone was seated (we redirected some students who selected places that weren't a good fit), we activated the timer and completed the checklist documenting students' behavior.

As soon as behavior occurred that didn't meet expectations, we called students back to the carpet. We asked them which guidelines they had been following, which they found challenging, and specifically what about their behavior had prompted us to end the independent reading session. (We asked them not to single anyone out by name.) They quickly decided it was because some students were talking. We discussed how difficult it is not to talk to our friends when we are reading a good book and assured them there would be other opportunities to do this during the day.

On a chart, we kept track of the number of minutes they spent reading independently. This first attempt lasted for four minutes. We asked them to try again and see whether they could improve their time, and they made it to five minutes. We continued charting their progress over the next few weeks, discussing things that were inhibiting and enhancing independent reading goals, until they were able to read productively for twenty minutes.

MONITORING AND REFINING

1. Continue to complete observational checklists.

2. Confer with students as needed to meet independent reading expectations.

3. Set goals with students as needed to maintain and support their independent reading experiences.

4. Hold discussions in which students introduce a book they are reading, discuss how they read it, and share whether they liked it.

5. Focus on enjoying and understanding independent reading.

Peek into Our Classroom

Our students quickly increased their stamina, and we were able to spend less time managing expectations and more time conferring with individuals. We completed a behavior checklist during each independent reading session and reviewed all five at the end of the week. When we noticed unsupportive behavior, we immediately conferred with the student exhibiting it, using our checklists as evidence. We asked the student why he thought this was happening and what he might do to make independent reading more beneficial. This often included reflecting on reading location and text selection. During the year, we periodically revisited the expectations and shared what we were noticing.

As routines became established, we shifted our focus to the ways we read. After independent reading time, we began to have classroom discussions about what book students were reading and the ways in which they were reading. We wanted to give students the power to be heard by their peers without our orchestration. We introduced supportive language frames ("Excuse me, [name], I'm ready to share," for example). During these discussions, the first student wishing to speak looked from student to student until he had everyone's attention. Then he introduced the book he read, talked about how he read it (reading the pictures; reading the words; retelling; or reading pictures, words, and design elements), and said whether he liked it. Then he asked another person to share or someone else volunteered, and the process repeated. Figure 3.10 shows William leading this process.

Although we emphasized the value of pictures and design elements in coming to understand a book, initial responses focused only on reading the words fast. During our first discussion, Aiden said, "I read *The Hungry Caterpillar*. I only read the words. I didn't like it because it's a baby book."

Meridith responded, "You *only* read the words? You didn't look at the pictures at all?"

"Nope. Only the words."

"Well, I think you should read it again, because the pictures are amazing. Tell me more about what you mean by it being a baby book?"

Figure 3.10 William leads the whole-class discussion group as he shares his new learning from his informational text. Cameron, Jordan, Mason, and Ava try to get a look at the picture in his book.

Aiden explained that it was an easy book, he knew all the words, and he thought it was for babies. When another student said, "I like that book," Meridith redirected the conversation, suggesting that just because a book is repetitive or easy to read doesn't make it a baby book or bad. She reminded students that the goal of reading is to enjoy and understand what they read, not just read fast.

Throughout the year, we continued to discuss students' experiences with texts and tried to privilege understanding and enjoyment over speed and accuracy.

DEEPENING

1. Identify strategies students are using to support meaning making with text.
2. Focus on decoding/fix-up strategies and comprehension strategies.
3. Identify strategies students are using to support their independent reading.
4. Highlight these strategies and have students share them with the class
5. Give students opportunities to discuss and reflect on the strategies they are using while reading independently.
6. Continue to monitor students' independent reading with the extended observational checklist.
7. Introduce reading response and self-selected inquiry opportunities to facilitate independence related to reading, responding, and sharing.

Peek into Our Classroom

As we observed students reading independently and listened to them talk about what and how they read, we helped them deepen their experiences and increase their independence by introducing fix-up and comprehension strategies (described in detail in Chapter 4). Figure 3.11 shows a student working during independent reading. We introduced self-selected strategies to support students' transactions with texts. Documenting this process required metacognition and resulted in engaging

Figure 3.11 James documents new information he learned during independent reading.

conversations about their independent reading that moved well beyond the four ways of reading and whether or not they liked the book. We added each student-initiated behavior to our checklist (Figure 3.12); the additions included making a connection, asking a question, making an inference, determining the author's intention, and using a fix-up strategy. A blank template is included in the appendices.

Will L.	Will C.	Valentina	Sophia	Shaun	Preston	Mason W.	Mason N.	Justin	Julia	Jordan	James C.	James (Jace)	Isha	Evan	Ethan	Emily	Christian	Chris	Cameron	Barrett	Ava	Alexis	Aiden	
																								Reading aloud
																								Reading silently
																								Tracking text
																								Pointing to pictures
																								Related talking
																								Looking at pictures/cover
																								Getting up
																								Staring at one page
																								Playing with book
																								Playing with other children
																								Unrelated talking
																								Seeking adult assistance
																								Making a connection
																								Asking a question
																								Making an inference
																								Author's intention
																								Using a fix-up strategy

Figure 3.12 End-of-year independent reading checklist

In addition to individual opportunities to deepen engagement with texts while independently reading, we also integrated response opportunities as a way for students to reflect on their reading and prepare for interactive opportunities to discuss their reading with peers. We introduced reading responses and self-selected inquiry projects that fostered independence related to reading, responding, and sharing. These response opportunities are discussed in detail in Chapter 5. Introducing and supporting strategies and response opportunities facilitated independence with a purpose for deeper reading and comprehension with a specific audience (peers or others).

ASSESSING PROGRESS

Our behavior checklist evolved throughout the year as students became more involved in and sophisticated about reading independently. Observation guided the instruction and support we provided to help students read independently, comprehend what they read, and deepen their reading experiences. Students' conversations and reflections about how they were reading, what they enjoyed about a book, and the strategies they used to help them understand what they were reading were a window into their independent reading experiences. Conferring with each student at least once a week helped us identify ways she or he was engaging with texts and the coaching or support she or he might need.

Considerations in kindergarten and second grade

	Teacher Modifications	Student Expectations
K	· Chart and build stamina up to 15 minutes. · Provide greater focus on "ways of reading" (pictures, design features, retelling, etc.). · Confer regularly to support approximated and conventional reading. · Emphasize fix-up and decoding strategies to support access to print.	· Build up to 15 minutes of independent reading. · Navigate books by reading the pictures, words, design elements and retelling familiar stories. · Discuss independent reading and strategy use. · Set goals for independent reading.
2	· Chart and build stamina up to 30 minutes. · Provide less focus on "ways of reading" (pictures, design features, retelling, etc.). · Confer regularly to support approximated and conventional reading. · Emphasize comprehension and interpretive strategies to support deeper meaning making.	· Build up to 30 minutes of independent reading. · Read picture books and chapter books. · Read pictures, words, and design elements. · Discuss independent reading and strategy use. · Set goals for independent reading.

Calendar

	Week 1	Week 2	Week 3	Week 4	Week 5	Week 6	Week 7-Dec.	Jan.	Feb.- June
Observational checklist	X	X	X	X	X	X	X	X	X
Introduce four ways to read a book	X	X							
Introduce building independence	X	X	X	X					
Track independent reading stamina	X	X	X	X (or until they reach 20 minutes)					
Introduce emergent decoding strategies	X	X	X	X	X	X	X		
Introduce comprehension strategies		X	X	X	X	X	X	X	X
Needs-based small groups				X	X	X	X	X	X
One-on-one conferring			X	X	X	X	X	X	X
Literature discussions					X	X	X	X	X
Reading response activities						X	X	X	X
Inquiry projects							X	X	X

4 · Strategies that Foster Independence

The children gather around our sharing space and quickly settle in for our first minilesson. We initiate the conversation by asking, "What do good readers do when they get to a word they do not know?" Hands shoot in the air. Farah thoughtfully states, "Good readers think about words when they don't know what they mean." Our hearts grow a little bigger. Yes, readers think about meaning! They must pause and consider one's understanding of the text. Farah is spot on.

We follow up with, "What strategies might you use if you realize you don't understand the word?" Within a matter of minutes, they discuss at least six different strategies that could be used to determine the meaning of an unknown word.

Claudia, a shy emergent reader, shares that you could chunk the word. Aubree chimes in with, "Read on and go back and see what would make sense." Dax confidently states, "You could make an inference." We press him with our three favorite words, "Tell me more." He replies, "Use your background knowledge and clues from the text to figure out the word." We are so excited about his use of the academic language.

The ping-ponging of ideas continues. Olivia eloquently describes using parts of a word to determine the meaning of a longer word. She refers to the word locomotion from Pout Pout Fish *(Diesen and Hanna 2008), declaring, "I know motion means to move, so locomotion must be something about moving." Landon pipes up in agreement, "Ya, like a train is a locomotive."*

Challenging his friends, Everett boldly states, "But, sometimes it doesn't work." We respond with, "You're right, Everett. Sometimes certain strategies don't work. That's why it's important readers have lots of good strategies to pull from." Then, Diego shouts, "Use the pictures," and the children grow a little louder as they all acknowledge the power of pictures. From the back, Olivia says, "But some books don't have pictures, like The Book with No Pictures.*" Finally, Aiden whispers, "Visualize, you could visualize what the word means."*

꙳ ꙳ ꙳

Strategy instruction is part of our everyday reading life. It is a continuous conversation. We don't just talk about visualizing in December and inferring in March. During whole-group, small-group, and conferring time, we revisit old strategies and introduce new ones. We use a common language to support and foster independence, and we always come back to the heart and soul of reading—meaning making. Through strategy instruction, we teach our students to think while they read, to interact with the text, and ultimately to become metacognitive readers who read to construct meaning.

One of the most frequent concerns about giving young readers extended periods of independence relates to their emergent literacy status. Teachers often worry the students don't yet have the strategies and skills to approach texts in meaningful ways. We utilize two different but related types of strategy instruction. We categorize our strategies for emergent reading as fix-up strategies or comprehension strategies. We hope that when students read, they will draw on all meaning-making systems and the strategic processing will become internalized and automatic. However, young readers often need supportive and explicit strategy instruction in what to do when they encounter difficulty figuring out words and/or understanding the story. We define fix-up strategies as strategies that help students decode and access challenging text. Comprehension strategies help students document and deepen their thinking about the text. Obviously, these two types of strategies are interrelated because many fix-up strategies rely on comprehension, and comprehension strategies often assist readers in figuring out words.

We share the general sequence we used to introduce the many options for strategy instruction in both categories, but it changes each year based on the students' needs. For example, the first year we worked together, our students needed a great deal of support with decoding and accessing the printed text, so we spent extra time introducing and revisiting fix-up strategies. The next year's students were strong decoders who needed more support with monitoring and deepening comprehension, so we spent little whole-class instruction on fix-up strategies.

A word of caution: We have seen too many classrooms where the lesson is the strategy of the week, every week, in the same order year after year, regardless of whether or not the students need it. Strategies should be introduced as the teacher identifies a need to help readers be more independent. The goal is not for students to demonstrate the strategy use for a grade or to document the ability to use strategies when prompted. Instead, they should use the most appropriate strategy to help them access and make meaning with texts. In the vignette, our first graders documented many strategies they would use if they didn't know a word. Their ability to talk about these strategies with ease is important, but our favorite part of this conversation was when Everett said, "But, sometimes it doesn't work!" He is absolutely right: sometimes they don't work, so students have to be exposed to many different strategies that might work in many different settings to be successfully independent with texts. As Duke (2014) and Keene (2008) note, strategies are a means to an end, not an end unto themselves.

• Supporting Research: Why Is It Important? Does It Really Work?

Proficient readers use a variety of strategies that include the semantic, syntactic, and graphophonic cueing systems (Bergeron and Bradbury-Wolff 2010; Buettner 2002; Clay 1991; McNaughton 1981). Clay's (1991) work with struggling readers in first grade focused on teaching them to use the multiple cueing systems to inform reading and to problem solve challenging words and miscues. The graphophonic cueing system is related to the visual cues of letters, endings, prefixes, and suffixes. When trying to get readers to activate this cueing system, teachers often say, "Does that look right?" The syntactic cueing system draws on the structure of language and grammar. "Does that sound right?" is frequently used in relation to the syntactic cueing system. The semantic system is directly related to meaning, so teachers might ask, "Does that make sense?" Proficient readers draw on all of these systems to monitor and self-correct when needed. Struggling readers often overly rely on the few strategies they know.

Every year, we have a few students who are challenged with reading independence because their go-to strategy of tapping out or sounding out every letter rarely works well enough to help make meaning of the text. Their reading often becomes laborious and focused on letters and sounds rather than word identification and meaning construction. It's our job to introduce additional strategies and support self-monitoring. First graders who received strategy instruction that supported the various cueing systems "were at the same levels of metacognitive knowledge as their peers in third or fourth grade, thus demonstrating the evidence that teaching students self-monitoring skills helped them close academic gaps between them and their peers" (Pratt and Urbanowski 2016, 561).

In addition to fix-up strategies including self-monitoring, proficient readers rely on multiple comprehension strategies. Pearson and colleagues (1992) summarized proficient readers as using the following strategies: making connections; asking questions; drawing inferences, determining importance; synthesizing information; and monitoring their understanding. Sensory imaging (visualizing) was added to the list by Keene and Zimmermann (1997). To support our readers in becoming independent and proficient, we introduced strategies as we observed a need. We highly recommend Jennifer Serravallo's (2015) *The Reading Strategies Book* as a reference for identifying appropriate strategies based on your students' needs.

Fix-Up Strategies

One of the most exciting things about teaching primary-aged readers is helping them become independent readers. They must be able to problem solve when they come to words they do not know (which happens frequently). Sounding it out doesn't always work, so we discussed, revisited, and introduced multiple strategies that might help them "fix up" the problems they encountered with unfamiliar words. We sincerely believe reading is more than decoding words, so we always emphasized word attack strategies accompanied with a focus on meaning making.

As always, the best way to foster independence is by providing individualized support for readers. This is particularly true with fix-up strategies. Some students have already internalized these strategies and might need little to no instruction in this area. Because of this, the context (whole-class, small-group, or individualized instruction) and order we teach these strategies varies from year to year. If the majority of the class is already proficient with these processes, we only spend time teaching and reinforcing these strategies in a small group. This was not the case for most of our first-grade classes, so we will share our instructional experiences and sequences in a typical first-grade year. Students feel successful and build confidence as they gain fix-up strategies that enable them to be independent.

PREASSSESSING

1. Document the miscues and strategies you notice students using when they encounter unfamiliar words when completing running records.

2. Analyze the running records for cueing systems: meaning/semantic (M), syntax/structure (S), visual/graphophonic (V).

3. Document patterns.

Peek into Our Classroom

We completed informal reading inventories with students at the beginning of the year. We documented and analyzed miscues and assessed comprehension at various levels of text difficulty. All our students were unable to employ an effective strategy to solve unfamiliar words (which varied in difficulty) on multiple occasions during the running record. There were very few self-corrections. We analyzed student miscues to determine which cueing systems students were relying on most frequently. These data influenced how we introduced other cueing system strategies. The students most frequently relied on meaning and visual cueing systems. Typically, our students would either sound out every sound and not consider the meaning or they would look at the picture and guess a word with few, if any, of the same sounds represented in the printed word. Our students needed support with self-monitoring and additional meaning and visual fix-up strategies.

TEACHING

1. Ask students to brainstorm strategies they use when they come to a word they don't know.

2. Write down the strategies on chart paper. See Figure 4.1.

3. Tell students the strategies you noticed them using during the running records.

4. Introduce one or two additional strategies based on your initial assessment.

5. Model getting stuck on a word during a read-aloud of an enlarged text.

6. Ask students to suggest which new strategy might help you figure out the word.

7. Model using the strategy.

8. Ask students to try using the strategy while they read the text with their partner.

9. Ask for examples of when the strategy worked and when it did not.

Peek into Our Classroom

We created a blank anchor chart with only the title "Strategies for Solving Words." We asked students to share strategies they used when they came to a word they did not know. They quickly listed off sounding it out, tapping the sounds, looking at the pictures, skipping the word, finding the parts they know, and chunking it. We explained that we wanted to build on the strategies they were already using but also use another strategy that would be helpful. We said, "Good readers use a lot of strategies to help figure out words. Good readers ask themselves three questions when they come to a word they are uncertain about: Does it look right? Does it sound right? Does it make sense?" We referenced a new anchor chart, Figure 4.2, with visuals to reinforce this idea.

We said, "I usually start with my favorite strategy. It is looking at the picture and using my background knowledge to guess." An enlarged text was projected onto the screen, and we modeled pausing and substituting *hen* for *chicken*. We referred to the anchor chart to revisit the questions, and students gave a thumbs up or thumbs down for each question. They accurately identified that it sounded right and made sense, but it didn't look right. We asked students for other strategies that might help us. Jose shouted, "Chunk it or sound it out!" We modeled trying to sound it out /c/ /h/ /i/ /c/ /k/ /e/ /n/, and the

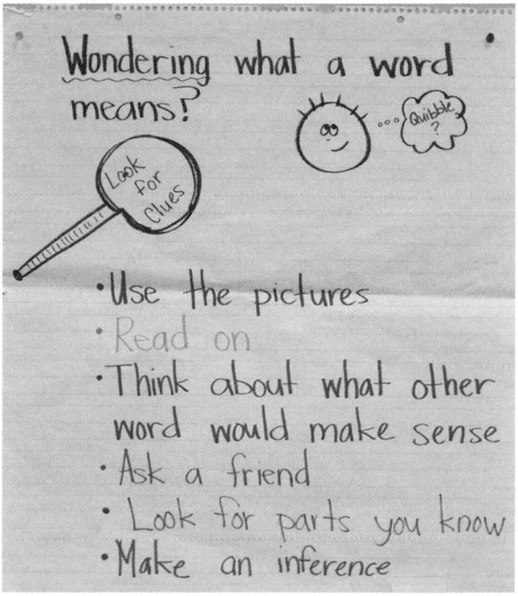

Figure 4.1 "Wondering What a Word Means?" anchor chart

Figure 4.2 "Ask Yourself . . ." anchor chart: Does it look right? Does it sound right? Does it make sense?

students laughed at our over exaggeration of sounding out each sound. We modeled finding chunks, solving the word, and rereading the sentence. We added the new strategy to the "Word-Solving Strategies" chart and asked students to try the strategy with their partner as they took turns reading. We encouraged them to use the questioning strategy when reading independently.

SCAFFOLDING

1. Review the "Word-Solving Strategies" chart.
2. Tell students to keep track of strategies they use to solve words because it will help them be more strategic and they can share their thinking with others.
3. Model using a strategy to solve an unfamiliar word. Write the strategy on a sticky note and place it below the word.
4. Ask students to continue this procedure with at least three words during independent reading.
5. Provide additional support as needed with conferring.
6. Debrief about strategy use with partner and whole-class sharing.
7. Connect to future partner and independent reading.

Peek into Our Classroom

We celebrated that students were able to identify multiple strategies when creating and reviewing the chart. However, we were perplexed because multiple students shared strategies we had never seen them use. They had been introduced to word solving strategies before and they could recite those strategies, but we wanted to build meta-cognition (thinking about their thinking) in relation to their use of fix-up strategies.

We documented our strategy use with skipping an unfamiliar word, reading on, and rereading the sentence. Using *Don't Let The Pigeon Drive the Bus!* (Willems 2003), we displayed the page with the text, "Hey, can I drive the bus?" We said, "'Hey, can I . . .' I don't know that word so I am going to skip it, read on, and come back to it with my mouth ready next time. 'The bus? Hey, can I /dr/, drive the bus?'" We wrote *skip it* on the sticky note and placed it under the word *drive*. We asked students to try this with three words they solved during independent reading. We observed that some students quickly and accurately used their sticky notes while other students struggled to use alternative strategies and document their thinking. We conferred with these students and supported them as necessary.

We asked the students to share their best strategy use and thinking with their partner. We called on volunteers to share their sticky notes, the strategy they used, and how they figured out the word. Alexis said, "I used chunking. See? *Anything* is a really big word I didn't know at first, but then I saw two chunks I did know. *Any. Thing.*" We encouraged students to continue keeping track of their best strategy use while they were reading independently and partner reading.

MONITORING AND REFINING

1. Continue observing students' use and documentation of fix-up strategies, and teach new strategies as needed. Here is a list of common fix-up strategies we introduced and used with the whole class:

   a. Use the words and pictures for clues.

   b. Tap it out.

   c. Look through the whole word.

   d. Chunk the word.

   e. Look for little words inside big words.

   f. Recognize sight words quickly.

   g. Flip the sound.

   h. Does it look right? Does it sound right? Does it make sense?

   i. Skip the word and go back.

   j. Reread for fluency.

2. During conferring and small-group time, ask students to tell you the strategies they could use to figure out words they are struggling to decode. Ask students how they successfully figured out an unfamiliar word they encountered while you were observing.

3. Identify students who need additional support and would benefit from a specific strategy.

4. Have the students bring their independent reading books with them to a strategy instruction small-group lesson.

5. Tell students you noticed them relying heavily on certain strategies. Explain that it is great to use those strategies, but they would also benefit from using the strategy you are going to teach/revisit today.

6. Briefly introduce/revisit and model the fix-up strategy they need and explain how this strategy will be helpful to them.

7. Ask students to try the strategy while they all read quietly to themselves.

8. Listen in to their reading, and coach as necessary with the strategy application.

9. Document students who use the strategy independently and ones who still require additional support. (Figure 4.3 is a strategy group note-taking guide sample. A blank template is in the appendix.)

	Chunk + reread without prompting.	Chunk + reread with prompting and support.	Alternative strategies tried
Strategy Group Goal: Chunk to identify words / reread to remember + build fluency			
Strategy: Chunk + reread			
Date: 9/30/2016			
Claudia	- inside (after initial coach)	- any way	- sounding out
Adan	stopped (after initial coach)	- asking	- look at pic -sound out
Leo	- kicking	NA-	
Kayla	-into (after initial coach)	cannot	- look at pic.

Figure 4.3 Small-group strategy note-taking guide

10. Have them write down the strategy with a visual representation on a sticky note to be used as a bookmark in their independent reading and partner reading experiences.

Peek into Our Classroom

After the first week of monitoring fix-up strategy use, we stopped prompting students to use a sticky note to document their fix-up strategy use. It remained an option, so students could document and share their fix-up strategy use in literature circle, with partners, in their reading responses, or in small groups. We continued to introduce or revisit some fix-up strategies with the whole class about once a week as necessary.

The assessment data (informal reading inventories, miscue analysis, conferring, and small-group reading) indicated we had a couple of small groups that would benefit from specific strategy instruction and reinforcement. Five students consistently relied on sounding out words without rereading. They would read an entire page that sounded like individual sounds, and they were unable to retell what they read. Another group would periodically look for letter clues, but typically looked at the pictures and guessed any word that made sense. These two groups of students needed separate and specific opportunities to apply appropriate strategies when reading. Because they needed support using opposite strategies, we provided this instruction in small groups.

We asked the students who were sounding out to bring one of their independent reading books to a small group. We said, "We noticed you have really been working hard on tapping or sounding out the letters when you are reading. This is a good strategy, and you can use it, but we also want you to be able to go back and reread the word. Sometimes we can't figure the word out with just sounding out, so I want you to look for chunks you know, reread the word to the end of the sentence, and then read the sentence again. This is going to help you do two things: It's going to help you remember the word, and it's going to help you read more fluently." We modeled this with two quick examples and asked the students to try it as we listened in. The minilesson on the strategy took less than two minutes. The coaching during reading took about ten minutes. During this strategy lesson with coaching, one student was able to apply the strategy without prompting and support. Three of the students initially tried sounding out and moving on, but were able to use the strategy with our coaching and prompting, and then used the strategy independently in the following unfamiliar word. One student was able to use it with prompting and support, but never used it independently. We documented this using the note-taking guide because we knew this child would likely need continued support.

After conferring with each child, we asked students to reflect on their use of trying to chunk and reread. Sarai said, "It's kinda hard to remember to do it. I still like tapping best." We replied, "We all have our favorite strategies, so it's hard to remember to try new ones. Let's make a little bookmark to help you remember to try this strategy during the week." We had them write the strategy title (*chunk and reread*) and create a visual/picture on a sticky note to use for their bookmark during the week. They also showed it to their partner so their partner could use it as a prompt during partner coaching.

EXTENDING

1. Review the fix-up strategies students have been using.
2. Ask students to document their fix-up strategy use during independent reading using sticky notes.

3. Explain they will be writing down and crossing out the strategies they tried that did not work. For example, if a student unsuccessfully tried sounding out the word *thinking*, then successfully tried chunking, they would write the following:

> Thinking
>
> ~~Sounding out~~
>
> Chunking

4. Model the process and ask students to try it during independent reading.

5. Give students a chart to document the strategies they used that worked and those that didn't work (Figure 4.4 was the model example).

6. Ask students to talk about what they noticed. Prompt with questions like, "Do you have a balance of strategies, or are you relying on one strategy? What strategies work for you? Which ones do not?"

7. Remind students that good readers use multiple fix-up strategies.

8. Have students set a goal about integrating a new and/or more effective strategy to help identify difficult words.

Peek into Our Classroom

Many students relied on two or three strategies to identify unfamiliar words. In general, these strategies were varied enough that students could eventually figure out most challenging words after a couple of attempts (in grade-level texts). However, we

Word	Strategies That Did Not Work	Strategy That Did Work
Thinking	Sounding out Look at the pictures	Chunking
Anything	Sounding out Skip the word and go back	Chunking
Goal: I will try to look for chunks or smaller words before sounding out.		

Figure 4.4

continued to observe students initially use the same strategy, like sounding out, even if it rarely worked. We wanted students to be more metacognitive about their fix-up strategy habits.

We had not talked about fix-up strategies in a whole-class setting for over a month, so we pulled out the fix-up strategy chart as a reminder of the previously discussed strategies. We said, "Fix-up strategies help us read, and today we want you to keep track of what strategies you are using, what is working, and what is not." We reminded them of the fix-up strategy sticky notes we used before, but explained we were "going deeper" with the fix-up strategy sticky notes. We modeled coming to the word *thinking*, attempting to sound it out, then finding chunks to figure it out. We asked students to turn and talk about what worked and what did not. They quickly identified the strategies, which we documented on a sticky note by writing the word and the strategies (crossing out the strategy that did not work). We asked students to try this with four words during their independent reading time.

After independent reading, we completed the chart in Figure 4.4. We said, "Good readers use a variety of strategies, but they pay attention to habits they develop so they know which strategies are working well and which are not. Let's take a look at ours. Hmm, it looks like chunking is really helpful for me, but I never use it first. I am going to set a goal for my reading this week to try to use chunking as my first strategy with big words." The students completed the table, and many seemed surprised about how often they first used the same strategy (most frequent was sounding it out) and how infrequently it worked. Loraina said, "I always tap it out first, but I need to think about if it makes sense or look at the pictures." We encouraged students to think about and connect their goals to their independent reading. We explained that we would revisit this exercise in two weeks to examine their progress toward the goal.

ASSESSING

We assessed students' progress with fix-up strategies in multiple ways. We first used our assessments and miscue analysis to analyze what cuing systems students relied on when they encountered unfamiliar words. The students' use of sticky notes to document strategy use in the beginning helped us determine whether or not they could articulate the strategies they were using. We assessed progress with fix-up strategy use during conferring, guided reading, and strategy-instruction small groups using detailed notes and note-taking guides.

The analysis of the strategies that were working versus those not working provided insight and assessment data. The self-assessment component often reiterated what we had been saying during strategy groups, but many students seemed to finally understand when they had the opportunity to self assess and set goals for themselves.

Considerations in kindergarten and second grade

	Teacher Modifications	Student Expectations
K	· Use images to reinforce strategies and help students remember them. · Use a common and consistent language for strategies. · Have students use colored sticky notes to document strategy (eliminate the writing requirement). · Provide reinforcement and needs-based instruction in small groups and conferences. · Modify number of strategies introduced. · Connect to independent reading with physical reminder (bookmark, sticky note, etc.).	· Use and identify familiar fix-up strategies. · Learn new strategies. · Document strategy use with colored sticky notes and/or oral language. · Apply strategies in small groups and conferences.
2	· Decrease instruction on traditional and simpler fix-up strategies. · Increase emphasis on strategies related to identifying syllables, word parts, prefixes, suffixes, root words, endings, and context clues. · Decrease instruction on fix-up strategies for students who no longer need it. · Provide reinforcement and needs-based instruction in small groups and conferences.	· Automatically use fix-up strategies. · Accurately name and/or document strategies used. · Learn and apply new and more complex strategies. · Analyze strategy use habits. · Decrease focus on fix-up strategies as reading becomes more proficient.

The following schedule below shows the initial introduction of strategies, but we revisit and monitor as needed throughout the year.

Calendar

	Week 1	Week 2	Week 3	Week 4	Week 5	Week 6	Week 7–Dec.	Jan.	Feb.–June
Administer/ analyze running records	X	X					X	X	X
Brainstorm fix-up strategies	X	X							
Introduce student strategy documentation				X					
Introduce using the pictures for clues	X								
Introduce tapping it out		X							
Introduce recognizing sight words quickly			X						
Introduce asking, "Does it look right, sound right, and make sense?"					X				
Introduce skipping the word and going back						X			
Introduce chunking the word/using little words inside big words							X		
Introduce flipping the sound								X	
Needs-based one-on-one conferring		X	X	X	X	X	X	X	X
Needs-based small groups and note-taking guide					X	X	X	X	X

James' nonfiction manatee book is filled with green "I learned" and blue "I wonder" sticky notes. He reads us a few. "I learned manatees are called sea cows. I learned manatees are omnivores. They have flat teeth, so you don't have to be afraid that they will bite you." James is stopping and thinking about his new learning. He's interacting with the text and absorbing new information. After sharing some of his green sticky notes, he turns to a page with a wonder sticky note. He frowns a little and reads, "I wonder why people are throwing trash in the ocean and hurting manatees?" This leads us into a discussion about saving the Earth and protecting wildlife. James is a very concerned and aware six-year-old. He is reading to learn about the world around him and questioning how to make it a better place.

Across the room, Valentina goes to the sticky note wall. She quickly grabs a pink sticky note and hurries back to her spot. She immediately starts writing. We lean over her shoulder and notice she is writing a character trait for Molly Lou Mellon. Her sticky note reads, "Molly Lou Mellon is brave because she doesn't let Ronald Durkin boss her around." Valentina's book is like a rainbow. She has pink, blue, orange, yellow, and purple sticky notes lining the pages that document her thinking during reading.

Our students are actively engaged with text. They aren't all reading quietly, but as we scan the room, we notice they are working with great intent. Some students are going to the sticky note wall, others are frantically recording their latest thought on a colored sticky note, some are peering over friends' shoulders checking out what they have written, and a few are whispering something to a neighbor and pointing in their book. They are thinking while they are reading and independently applying comprehension strategies to construct meaning. They are in charge of their learning.

🐾 🐾 🐾

Comprehension Strategies

Meaning making is at the heart of all of our literacy instruction. In the primary grades, many teachers emphasize "learning to read" over "reading to learn" (Chall 1983). We believe those two things have to happen simultaneously. Many students need additional support and strategies to become independent meaning makers of text. We introduced comprehension strategies to serve three purposes:

1. Help students acquire comprehension strategies that enhance their reading experiences.

2. Document their important thinking and use of comprehension strategies.

3. Share their thinking, meaning making, and strategic processing with others.

We were very cautious not to introduce a strategy a week and require all students to be using that strategy all week. Comprehension strategies support the characteristics of proficient readers who use specific strategies in specific contexts to support meaning making. Because of this, we did not always introduce these strategies in the same sequence, and sometimes we introduced multiple strategies in one week and none in others. Comprehension strategies provided a tool we believed students needed to become more independent and deepen their experiences with and discussions about texts. The sequence provided here is from one year; but note that the sequence of strategy instruction changes every year because we use our observations and formative assessment to guide our instruction in an organic way grounded in the students' immediate needs.

PREASSESSING

1. Analyze the informal reading inventories and running records to identify areas of need related to comprehension.

2. Document patterns of common challenges (retelling, making inferences, etc.).

3. Observe students during partner reading and discussion, conferring, and small-group reading to check for comprehension strengths and challenges.

Peek into Our Classroom

Our informal reading inventory assessments indicated that many of our students accurately decoded words but needed additional support with comprehension, specifically accurately retelling, self-monitoring, making connections, and making inferences. We asked students to share a brief overview of their favorite book from independent reading with their partner. We observed two common types of responses: a long, page-by-page description of what happened in the book or a very brief description. Both types of response technically fell under the instructions of giving an overview of the book, but we wanted to refine the way students talked about and thought about books when they were reading.

TEACHING

1. Create a chart with strategies students report they use to help them understand books.

2. Share strategies you observed them using.

3. Explain that good readers think and use strategies to understand the text while they read.

4. Introduce or review one to two additional strategies based on your initial assessment.

5. Model reading and thinking aloud with one to two strategies.

6. Ask students to use the strategy and share with a partner while you read the next section.

7. Encourage students to use this strategy when reading independently.

Peek into Our Classroom

Students told us that most of the strategies they used to help them understand books were directly related to decoding. We continued to prompt until Jordan said, "Well, I think about it when I am reading, like sometimes I think, I wouldn't do that!" This felt like a good place to start to encourage students to make connections to the text as a strategy for deeper engagement and self-monitoring. We said, "Yes! Good readers think about what they are reading and how it relates to their life and what they know. This is called a *connection*. It helps readers relate to the book, but it also helps us think about whether what we are reading makes sense." We showed students the connections anchor chart. We read aloud and made a connection to a feeling of a character in the book. We continued reading, asking students to make a connection and share it with a partner. We explained, "Sometimes it's hard to remember our thinking or connections when we are reading, so we are going to write it down so we can share it with our partner and discussion circle." We modeled using an orange sticky note and the language frame "This reminds me of _____." We told students not to worry about spelling, but just to take their best guess to get their thinking down. They practiced one connection as we continued the read-aloud.

We continued to teach each of the comprehension strategies as needed. We introduced the strategies and described how they could help students comprehend. The strategies were assigned a sticky note color. We included some type of sentence starter or qualification for what could be included. Figure 4.5 shows the language frames and strategy/sticky note options. We created an area on the cabinet with the strategy/sticky note description created by students with the color-coded sticky notes beneath. (See Figure 4.6.)

SCAFFOLDING

1. Review the previously introduced anchor chart.

2. Tell students to keep track of their strategy use with sticky notes (or whatever format you prefer) because it will help them be more strategic and thoughtful when

they are reading, and it can help them share their important thinking with other students and the teacher.

3. Ask students to document at least one instance of using the strategy during independent reading. If you have introduced multiple strategies, tell students they can also use those as necessary, but to try to document at least one example of the focus strategy.

4. Provide additional support as needed with conferring.

5. Have volunteers share their use of the strategy with the group followed by students asking questions, sharing comments, or making connections to the initial sharing (see a more sophisticated version of this in Chapter 7).

6. Debrief about strategy use.

7. Connect to future partner and independent reading.

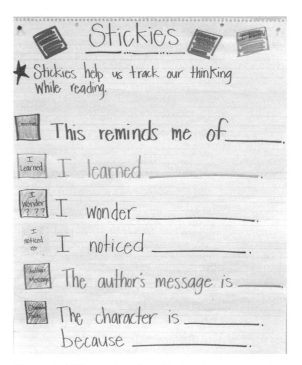

Figure 4.5 We continually added and encouraged the use of strategies. This chart provided a color-coded reference and language frames to help students document their strategy use.

Figure 4.6 Students created a title or label for each strategy. They included the name and gave a description of it in their own words to place above the sticky notes.

Students were excited about making connections because there was no right or wrong answer and it was guided by their own experiences. The first day we offered independent use of the sticky notes, it was total chaos. Everyone wanted to get as many sticky notes as possible. We actually had to stop independent reading because students were fighting over how many sticky notes other students had. It sounds silly, but it happened. In that moment of chaos and lack of learning, we broke our original rule of not putting requirements or numbers on strategies. We said, "Okay, no more than two orange sticky notes today. Just write down your best connections." We decided we could revisit expectations during the literature discussion circle.

There was a wide variety of connections. Emily pointed to a dog in a book and said, "There is a dog in this book. I have a dog." Kiley put the sticky note on a picture of a lion and wrote, "This reminds me of when we went to the zoo." Jenna put a sticky note next to a character who was being excluded and wrote, "This reminds me of when my brother was mean to me and I started crying." We called students back to the carpet to share their thinking. Kiley shared her sticky note, and students immediately started saying, "Me too. I went to the zoo." We got their attention again and asked Kiley to call on other students to ask questions or make comments or connections. After a couple of students shared their strategies, we asked them how they thought it went. Mika said, "I like it. It's like show and tell, but about the book." Sarah said, "Yeah, but only a couple people got to go." We agreed and told students they would also share their thinking and sticky notes with their partner today during partner reading.

MONITORING AND REFINING

1. Continue observing students' use and documentation of comprehension strategies and teach new strategies as needed. See the note-taking guide in Figure 4.10. (We eventually added these components to the observational checklist for independent reading.) Here is a list of common comprehension strategies we introduced with the whole class:

   a. visualizing

   b. sequencing

   c. five finger retell

   d. making connections (text-to-self followed by text-to-text and then text-to-world)

   e. pulling key ideas and details ("I learned")

   f. questioning ("I wonder")

g. character traits (Figure 4.7 uses purple to distinguish changing character traits.)

h. noticing

i. comparing and contrasting

j. making inferences

k. author's message

l. author's craft (Figure 4.8).

2. Encourage students to use self-selected and appropriate strategies without a specific requirement, number, or assignment. Explain that the strategies help students think while they are reading, and also provide a starting point for sharing their most important thinking with their peers.

3. During conferring and small-group time, ask students to talk about the comprehension strategies and how they help students understand the book (Figure 4.9).

4. Continue to ask students to share their most important thinking/strategy documentation during the literature discussion circle and partner reading.

5. Have students assess their strategy documentation in their reading response journal (more on this in Chapter 5).

6. Use strategy documentation as small-group literature circle discussion preparation.

7. Revisit, refine, and deepen strategy documentation and use as needed to support meaning making and conversation.

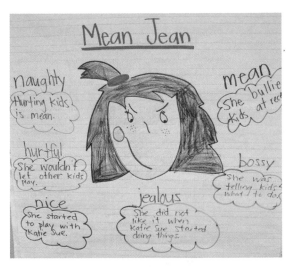

Figure 4.7 Students had many ideas about Mean Jean's character traits. We created this chart collaboratively and documented changing character traits in purple.

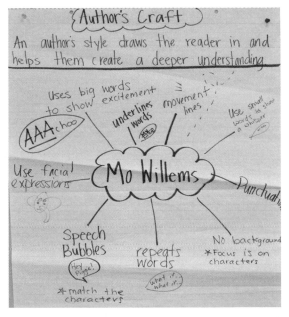

Figure 4.8 Students brainstormed many aspects of Mo Willem's craft. We documented their thinking to help with comprehension and writing.

	Visualizing	Sequencing	5 Finger Retell	Connections (TS, TT, TW)	I Learned (key ideas & details)	I Wonder	Character Traits	Noticings	Compare & Contrast	Inference	Author's Message
Aiden					S	S					
Alexis							M				M
Ava			M				M				
Barrett					S	S					
Cameron							M				M
Chris					S						
Christian			S								
Emily				M			-				
Ethan	None observed ⟶										
Evan				S	S						
Isha			S								
James					M	M					
James C.				I							
Jordan				S							M
Julia			M				M				
Justin					S						
Mason N.						S					
Mason W.					S	S					
Paul							I				I
Shaun				S							
Sophia							S				
Valentina							M				M
Will C.					M	M					
Will L.											S

I=Inaccurate Use, S= Surface-Level Use, M=Meaningful Use

Figure 4.9 Comprehension strategy checklist

After the first week of monitoring a specific strategy use, we no longer prompted students to use it. There was no specification to the types or numbers of strategy documentation. They were encouraged to document and share in the literature circles, partner readings, reading responses, or small groups. We continued to introduce or revisit comprehension strategies with the whole class as necessary. For example, in October, a small group of students participated in a discussion group and shared their strategy documentation and thinking. They had an excited conversation and referred to the text when Ava said, "I feel like we need another sticky note. This part is important, but it isn't really a question or what I learned." We asked, "What helped you think and talk deeper about the book? What would you call this?" Ava said, "It's like, I noticed." The other students agreed. This was a strategy we planned on teaching in a couple of weeks to the whole class, but the need for it arose, so we addressed it. The students created a sign and new sticky note color, and introduced it to the class.

The documentation was not perfect. Sticky notes were used excessively, and some documentations were surface level. We created an observational guide (Figure 4.9) to help us think about deepening and refining the strategy use. We didn't want students documenting strategies for strategies' sake; we wanted students to use strategies to be more metacognitive while reading and to facilitate deeper conversations. Our observational data indicated that students were using surface-level connections—things like "That tree reminds me of the tree outside" or "She has a brother, and I have a brother." We revisited the connections strategy and asked students to really focus on their best, "deep" thinking. We gave examples and nonexamples, but to make it more concrete, we asked students to write connections only related to feelings or themes. If the thought was something they could touch or see, then it probably was not their deepest thinking and not worth writing down. We explained that they needed to be able to justify how the strategy made them think and understand the book on a deeper level.

We asked students to challenge themselves and their partners by questioning their documentation of connections. This refinement also eventually moved into other strategies like documenting their learning, questions, and so on. We encouraged students to ask each other, "Why is that important? How does it help you understand? Can you go deeper with that?" These questions sparked more thoughtful conversations over time. However, some students were initially very disappointed as they discarded ten or twelve sticky notes when they did not pass the question test during partner reading discussions. Deepening and revisiting strategies changed the way students documented their strategy use. The conversations became less superficial. We found that refinement and revisiting never completely ended throughout the course of the year—they just changed by becoming revisiting and deepening instead of instruction and introduction.

EXTENDING

1. Review the comprehension strategies students have been using.
2. Show students the strategy reflection log graphic organizer (Figure 4.10).
3. Model removing colored sticky notes from a book and organizing them in the log. Explain that the types of strategies get more complex, and students need to make sure they are using a variety of strategies in their reading.
4. Have students complete a log with the strategies they used during their independent reading this week. Have them count the total number in each category.
5. Ask students to discuss what they noticed about their strategy use. Prompt with questions like, "Do you have a balance of strategies, or are you relying on one type? Are you doing enough deep thinking with inferring and analyzing?"
6. Have students set a goal about balancing their strategy use and only documenting their most important thinking. Have them continue to monitor their documentation.

	Strategy Documentation	Sticky Note (Evidence)
Summarizing	☐ Sequencing ☐ Five finger retell ☐ I learned (key ideas and details)	
Making connections	☐ Text-to-self ☐ Text-to-text ☐ Text-to-world	
Inferring	☐ Inference ☐ Character traits ☐ Visualize	
Analyzing	☐ Author's message ☐ Author's craft ☐ Compare and contrast	

Figure 4.10 Strategy Reflection Log

We told students we were impressed with their comprehension strategy use and documentation, and the way they used that to facilitate meaningful conversations with partners and small groups, but we wanted them to go deeper. We said, "Good readers use a variety of strategies to help them think about reading. We're going to analyze the types of strategies we use the most to make sure we have a good balance." We showed them the strategy reflection log graphic organizer in Figure 4.10 and asked them to help us organize the sticky notes we had in a book. The students quickly noted that we had many more sticky notes in the summarizing and making connections categories. When asked what categories required the deepest thinking and promoted the best conversations, they all agreed on the inferring and analyzing categories. Cameron said, "Probably character traits and author's message categories because we really have to think and give evidence. And, not everyone agrees, so we sometimes have to talk about it a lot and go back to the book to prove our thinking."

We agreed with Cameron and told students we noticed they were using a lot of strategies, and we wanted them to analyze their strategy use with the log. See Cameron's example in Figure 4.11. Most students had an abundance of sticky notes in the summarizing and making connections categories, but few in the inferring and analyzing sections. They discussed with a partner what they could do to deepen their think-

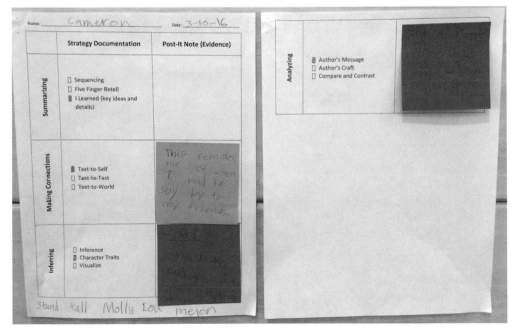

Figure 4.11 Cameron's sticky notes after reading *Stand Tall, Molly Lou Melon*

ing and maximize their strategy documentation. Aiden said, "I need to not write down so many I learned. I don't have anything in inferring and analyzing, so I need to do at least one." We asked each student to set a goal for creating more balanced strategy use and documentation to deepen their thinking and conversations about books.

ASSESSING

We assessed independent use of comprehension strategies in multiple ways. We first used our observations and informal reading inventories to identify areas of need related to comprehension. This helped us introduce strategies that supported making meaning with texts. Giving students sticky notes to document strategy use in the beginning let us know whether or not they were able to independently use newly introduced comprehension strategies. As the year progressed, we analyzed the individual strategy use according to levels of sophistication (inaccurate, surface, or meaningful). Finally, we assessed and asked students to self-assess their strategy use according to types of strategies and their complexity using the strategy reflection log. This allowed students to set their own goals for developing comprehension.

Considerations in kindergarten and second grade

	Teacher Modifications	Student Expectations
K	· Support comprehension with strategies through extensive oral opportunities. · Have students use colored sticky notes to document strategy (eliminate the writing requirement) and use as an oral prompt. · Encourage students to document thinking and strategy use with pictures/sketches. · Provide simple language frames to represent their thinking and strategy use. · Don't include the strategy analysis graphic organizer.	· Use strategies to reflect on and enhance comprehension. · Use oral language to share thinking and document use of strategies. · Document strategy use with colored sticky notes and/or oral language or drawing. · Apply strategies during small-group and conferring settings. · Use language frames to represent thinking and strategy use.
2	· Decrease instruction on literal comprehension strategies. · Increase emphasis on strategies related to inferring, analyzing, and critiquing with evidence from the text. · Provide opportunities for extended documentation of strategies such as justifying why they selected strategies and/or using sticky notes to prepare for a more formal response.	· Be familiar with many literal comprehension strategies. · Accurately name and/or document strategies they use. · Learn and apply new and more complex strategies. · Analyze their strategy use habits. · Use strategy documentation as a starting point for deeper responses.

The following schedule includes the introduction of strategies, but we continued to revisit and monitor as needed throughout the year.

Calendar

	Week 1	Week 2	Week 3	Week 4	Week 5	Week 6	Week 7–Dec.	Jan.	Feb.–June
Administer/ analyze running records	X	X					X	X	X
Brainstorm comprehension strategies	X	X							
Introduce strategy note-taking guide					X				
Introduce strategy reflection log								X	X
Introduce sequencing		X							
Introduce five finger retell			X						
Introduce making connections and using sticky notes				X	X				
Introduce "I learned" statements (key ideas and details)						X			

	Week 1	Week 2	Week 3	Week 4	Week 5	Week 6	Week 7–Dec.	Jan.	Feb.– June
Introduce "I wonder" statements (asking questions)							X		
Introduce character traits							X		
Introduce comparing and contrasting							X		
Introduce noticing								X	
Introduce author's craft								X	
Introduce visualizing									X
Introduce making inferences									X
Introduce author's message									X
Needs-based one-on-one conferring		X	X	X	X	X	X	X	X
Needs-based small groups					X	X	X	X	X

5 · Reading Response Opportunities that Foster Independence

Literature responses continue to be a work in progress. We used to have students respond to the same prompts every Friday. "What was your favorite book and why?" "Describe your favorite character." "Write about your connections." And every Friday we read statements like, "This book reminds me of my dog." "It is a good book because sharks are cool." "The pigeon is funny." These literal responses left us wondering how to make literature responses more meaningful. We knew something had to change, but it wasn't until Emily let out an audible "Ugh" when we announced it was time to write in our journals that we truly realized we needed to let go of mandatory Friday responses. Her reaction confirmed what we already knew—literature responses were not working.

Friday morning is still a time for reflection, but now children choose how they respond. They use their during-reading sticky notes to build upon and extend their thinking. Today, William is preparing a book talk for his classmates, while Emily joyfully creates her own version of the Three Little Pigs. *Barrett feverishly records all the new information he learned about volcanoes and poses unanswered questions. Ava analyzes her sticky notes to determine which ones reflect her very best thinking, and Cameron uses her sticky notes to write about the author's message in* The Recess Queen *and make connections to her own life.*

The choices are open ended because the response is a genuine interaction between the reader and the text. Each book elicits a different response or invokes a different emotion. Expecting the children to respond in the same way to different books sets them up to deliver low-level literal responses. Giving students more freedom and building upon their during-reading thinking allows them to go deeper and create meaningful and authentic responses to literature.

🐾 🐾 🐾

In this chapter, we introduce two types of authentic and meaningful response opportunities that support and deepen independent reading experiences. There are many ways students can respond to reading (both oral and written), but we focus on reading responses and inquiry projects. These two response opportunities facilitate independence and include individual and collaborative opportunities to document thinking. Response opportunities should serve multiple purposes including reflection, deeper thinking and/or strategy application, preparation for future discussions, and accountability/assessment. Response opportunities should not happen after every book, be busywork, or take more time than reading the book.

Our students used to keep book logs, but it often took first graders longer to write the title of the book than it did to read it. Keeping a book log isn't something we do as readers, so we eliminated it. We had students write reports about informational text, but we observed disengagement with a lack of purpose and authentic audience. We tried many different response opportunities, and we continued to ask ourselves, "How does this support students' meaning making and engagement with texts? Is this something real readers do?" If it didn't, we stopped doing it. Our students only submitted one "formal" response activity a week. This allowed them to enjoy their reading and prioritize the documentation of their best thinking related to fiction and narrative texts. These experiences ranged from using sticky notes to annotate thinking and prepare for discussions to conducting research and creating inquiry posters.

• Supporting Research: Why Is It Important? Does It Really Work?

Rosenblatt's (1978) transactional theory of reader response explores the relationship between the reader and the text. This theory positions the reader as an active participant, integrating personal response with the text to create the literary work of art. This theory resonates with us, and we wanted to facilitate and document these responses in meaningful ways. Hannock (1993) reported: "Although it has not been easy to capture and make sense of authentic, thoughtful response to literature, the written response to literature has gained support as a way of evidencing the transaction between the reader and the text" (336). Informal response journals are one effective way to document emerging reader response while connecting writing with the reading process (Bauso 1998; Blatt and Rosen 1984; Ruppert and Brueggeman 1986).

In addition to documenting and assessing the transactions, reading responses should provide opportunities to broaden students' understanding (Taberski 2000) and prepare them for conversations with partners and discussion groups (Moses, Ogden, and Kelly 2015). These opportunities increase student comprehension of text (Murphy et al. 2009). Response opportunities are often discussed in relation to narrative texts, but students also need opportunities for inquiry responses related to research topics of interest. Independent and collaborative inquiry increases engagement while simultaneously supporting language and literacy development in primary school English speakers and bilinguals (Moses 2011). Drawing on this research, we set out to foster independence with reading responses and inquiry projects.

Reading Responses

We grappled with reading responses in first grade for years. It was difficult to find a balance between the amount of time students should spend reading compared to the time they should spend responding. Daily logs and required responses to prompts felt contrived and time-consuming, not to mention that students viewed these as chores. Introducing a new focus for each response took time away from instruction and reading and did not always align with what they were independently reading; our students could never get into a routine and be independent. Yet not documenting learning and not responding robbed the students of time for reflection and took away a chance to prepare and share their important thinking. We simplified the process after trying and being discouraged with multiple response formats.

Like Flitterman-King (1988), we believed the informal nature of response journals allow students freedom to express their important thinking, rather than focus on supplying a "correct answer" or summary. It was difficult and time-consuming for first graders to go back and forth from reading to writing in a notebook. Instead, we encouraged students to document during-reading responses on sticky notes that could be placed in their journals and revisited at the end of the week. This allowed students to apply strategies, document important thinking, and prepare for discussion with input and choices for how they demonstrated their learning. These responses connected strategy instruction (Chapter 4), partner opportunities (Chapter 6), and small-group experiences (Chapter 7). The written responses became part of their interactive opportunities with partners and small groups. This integration and independence came with time and a great deal of scaffolding based on observations and formative assessment.

PREASSESSING

1. Informally assess the following:

    a. students' during-reading responses to text, orally and on sticky notes (introduced in Chapter 4)

    b. prompted postreading response with specific focus such as strategy or theme (summary, retell, author's message, and so on)

Table 1

Reading Response Note-Taking Guide

	During Reading		After Reading	
	Strengths	Needs	Strengths	Needs
Claudia	-Fix up -chunk	-more focus on comp.	Didn't	Complete
Adan	-NF text -?s -I learned	-summarizing	-accurate information	-Put in his own words
Leo	-NF text -?s -I learned	-prioritize thinking/ stickies	-Many stickies	-Focus on big ideas + importance
Dax	-Connections	-go deeper -prioritize	-Author's message	-Supporting evidence
Evelynn	-Fix up -chunk -reread	-Comp strat	-Author's message	-Supporting evidence

Figure 5.1

2. Observe students and analyze documents using the Reading Response Note-Taking Guide (Figure 5.1). A blank template is supplied in the appendix.

Peek into Our Classroom

In the beginning of the year, students completed self-initiated reading responses during reading (based on strategy instruction explained in Chapter 4) and teacher-prompted responses once a week after reading. Students completed a teacher-prompted response in their journals on Fridays, which we used to provide grades/accountability for students' independent reading. These ranged from identifying their favorite book with supporting reasons to documenting a text-to-self connection. We needed more information. We created the note-taking guide to help focus our informal assessment. The initial results were mixed.

We observed many strengths during reading responses. Students self-selected and documented appropriate strategy use for both fix-up strategies and comprehension strategies. Many of these responses were used to initiate important conversations about texts with their partners, small groups, and the class. However, some students had multiple sticky notes on every page. These students needed to prioritize their thinking and documentation because their current responses were often surface-level and interrupted reading flow; they were spending more time writing than reading.

Unfortunately, the postreading responses indicated very few strengths and some significant needs. In all honesty, the responses were surface-level busywork. Students were documenting strategies we introduced, but it was prompted by us, and students weren't thinking deeply or participating in meaningful conversations. This assessment helped us rethink how we could deepen students' during- and after-reading responses and connect them to the social context of thinking and talking about reading.

TEACHING

1. Share your observations about reading responses with your students.

2. Set goals for prioritizing documentation and responses that deepen thinking, facilitate conversation, and can be used by students as preparation for literature discussion groups and partner discussion.

3. Model analyzing sticky notes from during-reading responses.

4. Select your best thinking with three sticky notes to place in your reading response journal.

5. Explain why you selected the sticky notes (emphasize interpretation and opportunities for conversation).

Peek into Our Classroom

We told students, "We noticed some of you are using a lot of sticky notes. We are excited you are using your strategies and want to share your thinking with us and your classmates. Good readers don't just write down every thought that comes to their head. They write down the most important thinking. We want to see your most important thinking, so we are going to show you how to help narrow it down. Remember when we talked about going deeper with connections? We are going to try to do that with all of our strategies. Watch what we do."

We showed students our copy of *Stand Tall, Molly Lou Melon* (Lovell 2001) that was overflowing with sticky notes on nearly every page. The students were familiar with the story, so we told them we were going to "analyze" our sticky notes by categorizing them into two columns, titled Literal or Deep. We explained, "Literal responses are information that comes right from the text, and they aren't very good for conversations. In deeper responses, readers use the text and their own thinking to make inferences. Deep responses are good conversation starters because everyone can talk about their thinking and bring different ideas." We asked students to help us categorize our sticky notes from *Stand Tall, Molly Lou Melon* (Lovell 2001).

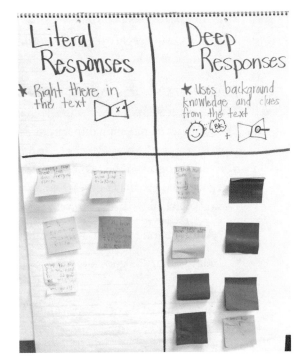

Figure 5.2 Students helped us analyze our sticky notes into literal and deep responses as we created a new anchor chart.

The first sticky note said, "I noticed Molly is short." Students did a think-pair-share and unanimously agreed that sticky note went in the Literal column (Figure 5.2). We continued analyzing the remaining sticky notes. Then we explained that we wanted to document our best thinking in our reading response journal each week, so we needed to select three sticky notes. These three sticky notes would be used to document strategy use, to start conversations with partners, and to prepare for literature discussion groups. We asked students to identify their three best sticky notes, and they selected a character trait with supporting evidence, an inference, and an author's message. When asked why they selected these, Cameron said, "Because they have the most to talk about. Like, I agree with them, but I also have something else to say about it."

SCAFFOLDING

1. Review the criteria for analyzing and selecting sticky notes.
2. Ask students to work with partners and separate sticky notes into two columns, titled Literal or Deep.
3. Have students select their three best sticky notes to place in their reading response journal.
4. Debrief with students about analysis and selection.

5. Set goals for upcoming responses.

6. Continue weekly reading response entries with additional conferring and support as needed.

We asked students to review the T-chart with the Literal and Deep columns. We said, "We practiced analyzing our thinking on sticky notes, now we want you to do it with a partner. Select a book you believe has your best thinking documented, and organize your sticky notes in the two columns." Students quickly met with their partners and categorized their sticky notes. Some students only had one or two sticky notes that could be placed in the Deep column. We overheard the following conversation:

Ava: That one goes in the Literal column!

Justin: No, it is good for conversation. Everyone wants to talk about deadly predators.

Ava: Yea, but it isn't deep. You just wrote down information from the book. She said it had to be from the book and your own thinking or inference.

Justin agreed and placed the sticky note in the Literal column. Most students negotiated with their partner and easily analyzed their thinking. We then asked students to create an entry in their reading response journal, place their three best sticky notes inside, and share their selections with their partner. We called them together and asked them how it went. Ava said, "Great! It was fun to look at all my sticky notes and pick the best." Sarah said, "Okay. I only have one deep response." We responded, "That's okay, for now, you can just choose two that you think are strong from the Literal column. We are looking at our thinking to pick our best, but also to help us set goals for upcoming responses. Your goal might be to have at least three deep-thinking sticky notes to place in your response journal by the end of the week." We asked everyone to set a goal for their reading response for the following week. Alexis shared, "My goal is to have four deep-thinking sticky notes so I can just pick the best ones." We suggested students kept this goal in mind while they completed their during- and after-reading responses during the next week.

MONITORING AND REFINING

1. Continue reading and providing feedback as needed on students' reading responses.

2. Use reading responses as preparation for whole-class and small-group literature discussions (explained in depth in Chapter 7).

3. Use the more sophisticated graphic organizer for analysis of strategies found in Chapter 4 because students have more types of thinking and strategy documentation to analyze.

4. Identify areas of need for deepening thinking and documentation of thinking.

5. Introduce additional response opportunities.

Peek into Our Classroom

On a weekly basis, students documented their best thinking by selecting sticky notes for the reading response journal. This became an easy independent routine on Fridays prior to their book talks and book shopping. Reading their response journals provided us with examples of their during- and after-reading thinking and strategy use and their views on what constitutes their best thinking. We used these data and observations of their discussions to identify areas of need. Some students needed to revisit certain strategies, such as deepening connections and providing supporting evidence for character traits. We moved beyond the T-chart to the strategy documentation graphic organizer because students were ready for a greater challenge related to strategy use and documentation. Students independently completed this reading work during and after reading daily, and they analyzed and compiled on Friday. They took responsibility for their self-selected documentation, reflection, and goal setting related to their reading responses.

We continued to add strategies and provide response opportunities that included critique and more-sophisticated thinking. Then, that response option became part of the independent options for responding. When we selected a specific response to reading, it had to have an authentic audience and purpose. For example, we wanted students to begin critiquing literature, so we made it part of our preparation for a book awards celebration (more on this in Chapter 7). After generating categories for book awards, students had the option to craft an argument with supporting evidence to present to their peers about the book they thought should win. See the example in Figure 5.3.

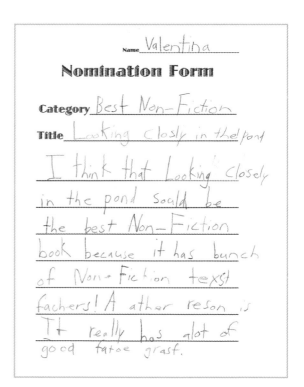

Figure 5.3 Valentina loved *Looking Closely Around the Pond*. Her nomination includes supporting reasons and evidence.

The expectations and routines became an automatic daily and weekly experience for students. Students were accountable for documenting their learning. Responses enhanced their reading and thinking, instead of taking time away from it. Students had choice in what they submitted for their weekly reading response, but they had to turn in some documentation of their best thinking.

EXTENDING

1. Review the "Author's Craft" anchor chart.
2. If not previously mentioned during writing workshop, discuss the idea of mentor texts and authors.
3. Explain that writing using an author's craft shows a deep understanding of what was read as well as the application of students' own thinking and ideas.
4. Introduce writing as a new option for postreading response on Fridays.
5. Provide opportunities for sharing, feedback, and publishing.

Peek into Our Classroom

We loved Lisa Cleaveland's work with first graders in *More About the Authors* (2016). We wanted our students to take up her idea of deeply reading and being inspired by authors. This inspired writing required students to move beyond analysis and critique to creation, design, and appropriation of author's craft. We thought this was the ultimate reading response documentation of meaning making and beyond!

We reviewed Mo Willem's "Author's Craft" anchor chart and explained, "Mentor texts or mentor authors help us become better readers and writers. Authors are inspired by other authors. To write like another author, we have to read the book really closely and think about how we can use some of the author's craft to make our own story." We told students that "inspired writing" would become an option (if they wanted to) for the submitted reading response on Fridays.

The first week, many students wrote stories inspired by Mo Willems. Farah's writing (Figure 5.4) had sad faces on the top of the first page and happy faces with one pigeon on the top of the last page. We asked her to talk to us about her story, specifically the sad and smiley faces, and she said, "Well, these are sad faces because Mo Willems always gives the reader a clue about how the character is feeling in the beginning in the endpapers at the front of the book. He does the same thing with how they feel at the end at the back. And, he always hides a sneaky pigeon in there somewhere!" We were impressed with her use of image, design, and written text to document her understanding of the genre and author. However, we also realized students might need more booklike formats for writing so they could create things like their own title pages and endpages. We switched to a book format as seen in the Jon Klassen–inspired book in Figure 5.5. Students could place

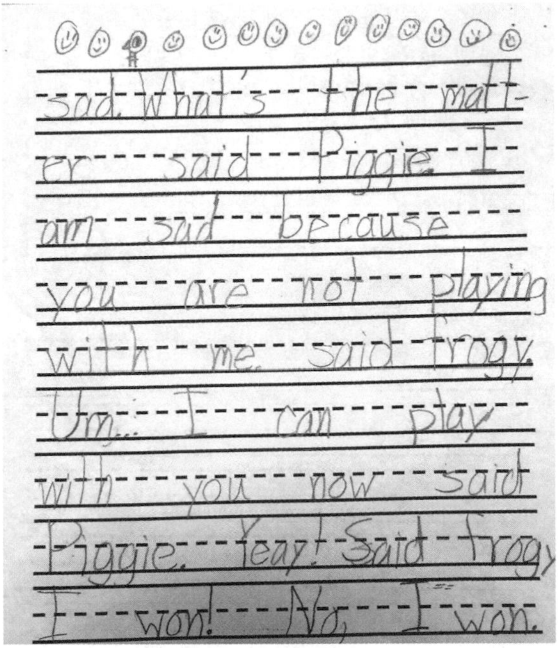

Figure 5.4 Farah created her own endpages at the top of her writing. Her inspiration was Mo Willems.

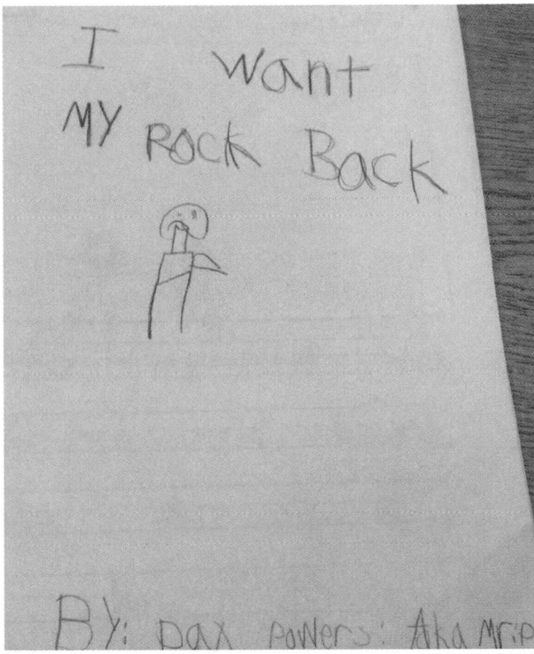

Figure 5.5 Dax published a book inspired by Jon Klassen with similar font, image, and design style.

their book in their reading response journal as their selected weekly submission. We gave students opportunities to share during partner reading and small groups. If they decided to continue working on the writing and publish it, it became part of our classroom library of books authored by students, or they could keep it in their reading box. These reading responses helped students think more deeply about texts, provided opportunities for discussion and engagement about their thinking, and gave students independence and choice in how they documented their meaning making.

ASSESSING

We observed students while they completed their reading responses and provided immediate feedback, as needed. Initial observations were related to students' during-reading responses, analysis of responses, and discussion of sticky note selection with partners. During the selection of sticky notes, students also participated in a self-assessment as they analyzed and selected their best thinking and set goals for improving their next reading response.

We collected reading response journals on Friday to read and provide feedback. This informal assessment provided information about students' use of strategies, analysis of their strategy use, documentation of critique, and understanding and appropriation of writer's craft. This documentation over the course of the year was used as part of their reading grade and was shared with parents during parent-teacher conferences. See Figure 5.6 for the rubric we used for grading these responses. At the end of the year, we asked students to go back through their reading response journals and reflect on how they had grown as readers since the beginning of the year. These concrete examples facilitated thoughtful self-reflection about their progress in reading and responding.

Needs Additional Support (.5 points)	Approaching Expectations (1 point)	Meets Expectations (2 points)	Exceeds Expectations (3 points)
3 literal (or less than 3 responses)	1 deep 2 literal	2 deep 1 literal	3 deep

Figure 5.6

Considerations in kindergarten and second grade

	Teacher Modifications	Student Expectations
K	· Create graphic organizers or specific format for visual or oral responses to reading in the beginning of the year. (Responses could include selecting a favorite book from the week, sketching a picture, and orally sharing with a partner why they liked it.) · Introduce modified colored sticky notes to mark their documentation of thinking (fix-up strategy, simple comprehension) by color without writing. · Extend responses to writing with sentence starter documentation as the year progresses.	· Use oral or sketched responses to document thinking during and after reading. · Select best thinking to include in reading response journal. · Create written responses with the support of a sentence starter.
2	· Introduce prolonged use of strategies and documentation (like charting character changes over time in chapter books). · Provide more extensive instruction for deeper comprehension strategies. · Introduce opportunities for critique and analysis responses and dialogue. · Introduce the analysis of writing and authorship across multiple texts, genres, and so on for inspired writing opportunities.	· Read more complex text that extends reading for over a week. · Document reading responses throughout extended texts by using deeper comprehension strategies to analyze change over time in chapter books. · Use complex comprehension strategies like analysis and critique. · Collaborate with peers to analyze strategy use and documentation. · Complete inspired writing pieces of increasing length and attention to detail.

Calendar

	Week 1	Week 2	Week 3	Week 4	Week 5	Week 6	Week 7–Dec.	Jan.	Feb.– June
Introduce during-reading responses, sticky notes				X					
Assess during-reading responses				X	X	X	X	X	X
Introduce analyzing during-reading responses								X	X
Introduce mentor text responses								X	X
Introduce critiquing responses						X	X	X	X
Assess reading responses (Fridays)						X	X	X	X
Needs-based small groups					X	X	X	X	X
One-on-one conferring				X	X	X	X	X	X

Our first graders scatter across the room to work on their arctic research project. It's busy and messy in the classroom. The mess alone may scare off some, but not these kids and not these teachers. We embrace it because this work is important. The students are research experts, and to us, this organized chaos produces its own natural flow and independence. It includes the shuffling of feet as students hurry to gather supplies, the swooshing of crayons over poster board, the rapid turning of pages as they search for big ideas, the peeling of sticky notes, the tapping of pencils, and the wandering of eyes followed by gasps of inspiration. The energy in the room is electrifying!

Shaun and Cameron co-research arctic foxes on the computer. Cameron shouts, "Shaun, arctic foxes can have a litter of six to twelve pups. That's a lot of babies. Our book didn't tell us that." They both write this new learning on a sticky note and add it to their research file.

Christopher sprawls out on the floor, crayons all around, papers stacked up ready to be glued on his poster board. He is a walrus expert. His poster is set upon the background of a giant walrus, just a few feet shy of life size. Valentina, another walrus expert, tells him she really likes his walrus background, and asks if he needs help filling in the white space. She grabs a brown crayon and joins in.

Lacie pulls sticky notes out of her snowy owl book and organizes her big ideas. She waves us over, holds up two sticky notes, and states, "I think these big ideas go together, but I'm not sure." She reads us her sticky notes, "Snowy owls eat up to five lemmings a day. They use their sharp talons to catch prey." We respond with, "What do you think?" She replies, "Yes, because they are both about what they eat and how they get food." We shake our heads in agreement, she smiles, and jumps back into her book.

We ring the chimes and it's time to clean up. The children let out a united, "Noooooo." There is a lot to clean up, but Mason cannot resist showing off his arctic fox poster to all his friends. He's so proud of his detailed information, colorful title, and realistic diagrams. He can hardly contain himself and neither can we.

Inquiry projects are a labor of love for students and teachers. The students must understand that becoming an expert requires perseverance, dedication, and time. It means taking your learning to the next level and sharing your expertise with others. Inquiry projects create a sense of purpose and ownership that encourages students to keep wondering, creating, and learning. For teachers it requires patience, faith, and flexibility. As Socrates reminds us, we must step back and let the children guide their learning. In doing so, we are reminded that education is not the filling of a vessel, but the igniting of a flame.

🐾 🐾 🐾

Inquiry Projects as Informational Reading Responses

To encourage deeper responses and engaged reading with informational texts, inquiry projects seemed like a logical next step because they increase comprehension and motivation with informational texts (Moses 2011). We were unsure how to move students beyond a culmination of facts on sticky notes that they documented during independent reading to a cohesive inquiry project. Some of our favorite resources for supporting inquiry helped shape our thinking—that it is about the curiosity and process, rather than just the final product (Buhrow and Upzcak-

Garcia 2006; Heard and McDonough 2009; Harvey and Daniels 2009). In full disclosure, inquiry is messy. It includes multiple sources, collecting information, putting information together in meaningful and aesthetically pleasing ways, and presenting and sharing expertise. It can initially feel untenable to assist students with so many different needs researching different topics. We began to work toward inquiry from the beginning of the year with an emphasis on comprehending informational text and documenting new learning. Once we felt comfortable with students' engagement with informational texts, we introduced small steps for independent inquiry within expert groups followed by co-researching opportunities. Eventually, students had the opportunity to participate in completely self-directed inquiry projects. To identify the necessary supports, we had to first examine how students were responding to informational texts.

PREASSESSING

1. Build background and interest about a topic/theme.

2. Ask students to self-select an area they would like to research (begin with options that fall within a familiar theme or content area).

3. Help students select multiple texts on the topic.

4. Prompt students to document their thinking during and after reading.

5. Ask students to share their responses with other students who chose the same topic.

6. Document the type of talking and interactions that take place during and after reading. See the open-ended note-taking guide sample in Figure 5.7. A blank template is provided in the appendix.

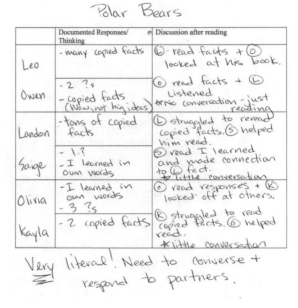

Figure 5.7

Peek into Our Classroom

Reading responses with narrative texts were strong, but we wanted to deepen students' response experiences with informational texts. We told students they were going to become experts on an arctic animal of their choice. We read aloud various informational books and brainstormed lists of polar animals they might be interested in researching. Then, students documented their questions and background knowledge about polar habitats on sticky notes and placed them on a poster. We used this information to create a sense of intrigue and investment before selecting their inquiry topic. We presented them with a list of options, and the students signed up for the animal they wanted to study.

Students spent their independent reading time reading informational texts on their topic and documenting their thinking and learning on sticky notes. Then, students met to discuss their thinking and learning with peer "experts" studying the same animal. Students who were the only person in their group were partnered with another small group. As students shared their responses, we heard an excessive amount of fact sharing and questions. Many of the facts were interesting, but only mildly related to their topic.

TEACHING

1. Discuss how experts share observations.

2. Explain that experts read, research, and document their learning over long periods so they can bring together the most important information.

3. Generate a list of essential questions and ideas students think are needed for the research projects. Turn this list into a bookmark/checklist for students. See the example in Figure 5.8.

4. Share the research project requirements. See the example in Figure 5.9.

5. Set up an organizational framework for collecting information and preparing the final project/product. See Figure 5.10 for an example inquiry folder.

Big Ideas
Arctic Animals

- Where does your animal live?

- What does your animal look like? (special features, color, length, weight, body parts)

- What does your animal eat? How does it get food?

- How does your animal survive in the cold?

- What does your animal do?

- What are the babies like?

- Other interesting facts.

Figure 5.8 This bookmark/checklist included the essential questions and ideas for students' research project. They also used it to question, discuss, and give feedback during partner conversations.

Arctic Animal Research Project

Title	Title is clearly written and easy to identify.
3 Big Ideas	Includes 3 big ideas. Each big idea is answered with at least three well-written sentences.
2 Non-Fiction Text Features (picture with a caption, diagram, map, glossary)	Non-fiction text features show new and interesting information. They also support big ideas. Illustrations are a level four.
2 Wow Facts	Includes two interesting or surprising facts about your animal.
Accuracy	All information should be factual.
Neatness	Neat handwriting. Organized presentation. Colorful.

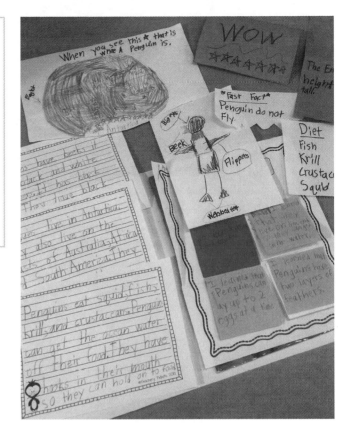

Figure 5.9 The minimum requirements for the inquiry research. Most students went far beyond, but these helped guide students' initial thinking.

Figure 5.10 Ava's inquiry folder during the information gathering and preparation stage. Students read extensively, gathered information, and documented their thinking through visuals, lists, and writing.

Peek into Our Classroom

We noticed that students collected a lot of facts and questions. We said, "Experts ask a lot of questions and gather a lot of information. So that is a great place to start. We need to think about what experts do. What do they need to know? How would they present it?" We explained that they were going to become experts and share their information on posters with a presentation for their peers. Their expertise was very important because that is how the other students would learn about the rest of the arctic animals. We brainstormed a list of "big ideas" that they thought everyone would need to know about each of the animals and wrote the list on an anchor chart. We typed it up that night and gave it to students as a bookmark/checklist the following day.

We showed students an example of a previously completed poster. Students shared things they noticed on the poster. All of these were components that we had discussed and used before (images, captions, summaries, nonfiction text features, maps, and so on). We gave students an inquiry folder to store their books and documentation. Inside, we glued the guidelines for the arctic research project. We said, "Research takes a long time, and we won't be done in a week for our regular Friday reading response.

A lot of parts go into making a good research poster, so you can collect them in this folder. Once you have checked off all the requirements, you can begin putting your large poster together."

SCAFFOLDING

1. Review the inquiry project requirements and big ideas handouts.
2. Give students a graphic organizer for organizing their sticky notes related to the big ideas (Figure 5.11).
3. Have students work on independent inquiry projects during independent reading.
4. At the start of partner reading, have students discuss their inquiry projects and progress.
5. Confer with individuals and expert groups.
6. Ask students to share their research progress on Fridays with their expert groups.
7. Provide additional support as needed with conferring.
8. Create small- or whole-group presentation opportunities.

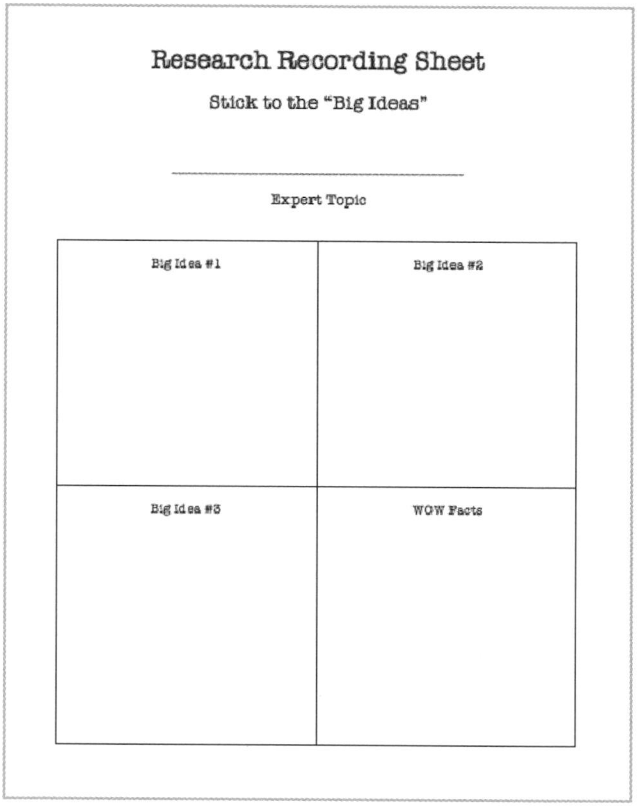
Research Recording Sheet

Stick to the "Big Ideas"

Expert Topic

Big Idea #1	Big Idea #2
Big Idea #3	WOW Facts

Figure 5.11 Research sticky organizing sheet.

Peek into Our Classroom

We worried there would be too many things to manage, so we created a graphic organizer to help students compile their sticky notes related to the big ideas. The students were eager to begin collecting information. Some students needed the additional support of listening to information (on the computer, a book on tape, or read aloud by us) because the texts were challenging. We provided this type of support and discussion during conferring and small groups.

Students enjoyed sharing their new learning with their partners at the start of partner reading each day. We asked them to check off requirements with their partner when they had been accomplished and shared. During the first week, we were surprised that almost all our students read and collected information on sticky notes without using images or nonfiction text features. We reminded students that they should document their thinking in various ways. We shared Evan's paw diagram from Figure 5.12 and asked students to talk about the various requirements his diagram addressed. Shaun said, "That is cool! It has how it gets food, what it looks like, and how it survives in the cold." Ethan added, "And what it does, and it is a non-fiction text feature."

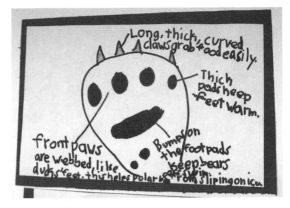

Figure 5.12 Evan's paw diagram included labels and the purpose of each part of the paw. The diagram answers more than one essential question in just one diagram.

Students met on Fridays to share their research progress. These meetings involved making connections, sharing resources, and helping each other find additional information. As students completed their inquiry posters, they had opportunities to present to other small groups of students who were from a different expert group. Jordan was one of the first presenters (many students were still working on their research) and she presented on her expert topic of polar bears. She asked for questions, comments, or connections. Aiden looked horrified and said, "Wait, so your animal kills my animal?" Jordan started giggling and responded, "Yep, I am the expert on your animal's predator!" We said, "Wow, it looks like Jordan's presentation is giving you additional information for your research poster on seals." Aiden added the information to his inquiry folder.

We collected students' inquiry folders on Fridays. This counted as their formal reading response for the week. We provided feedback as needed on the folders. Our weekly review of their inquiry work guided the conferring and small-group sessions for the following week. As students finished, they began a new inquiry project or they returned to other reading response options.

MONITORING AND REFINING

1. After your students are able to work independently on their inquiry projects, introduce an opportunity for co-researching and collaborating on self-selected topics within a specific system/topic.

2. Introduce a new format and requirements for the inquiry project (lap book, TED talk, wiki, video, and so on).

3. Create a chart about expectations for co-researching. (See Figure 5.13.)
4. Have students work on co-researching projects during partner reading time.
5. Use the co-researching note-taking guide in Figure 5.14 for observations. This is a modification from the original inquiry note-taking guide.
6. Confer with groups as needed.
7. Groups present their projects to the class.
8. Research groups collaborate to make murals that are representative of their collective understanding of the larger system or topic (solar system, ocean, habitats, and so on).
9. Display research projects and murals.
10. Allow students to continue co-researching with self-selected topics and formats.

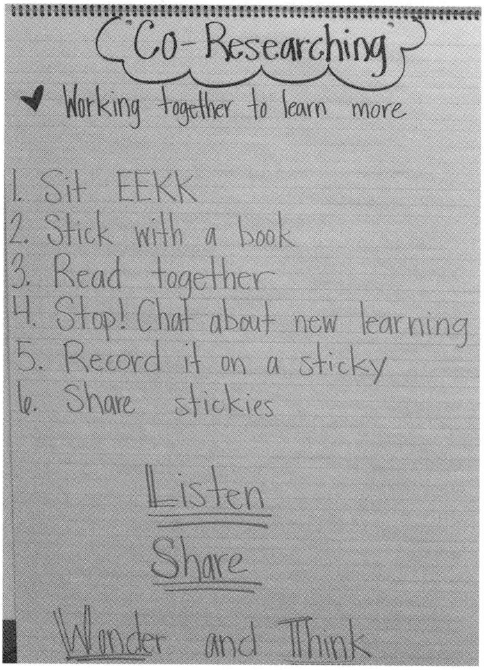

Figure 5.13 This co-researching anchor chart includes the purpose and procedures.

MARS

Inquiry Response and Interaction Note Taking Guide

		Documented Responses/ Thinking	Discussion During Reading	Discussion After Reading
WK1	Jordan	★Ava did all the writing ↓	- identifying important info. - negotiating big idea info. - equal participation	- reread responses
	Ava	- 2 big ideas - 3 I learned - 2 ?s		★Coached on need to check in on progress + needs for upcoming work
WK2	Jordan	- 3 Wows - 2 big ideas - 3 I learned	- making conn. across texts - documenting + organizing important info. for lapbook	- organizing new learning - realize they have conflicting facts
	Ava	★Jordan did the writing		★Coached on finding additional sources
WK3	Jordan	★Ava wrote, but both shared ideas. ↓	- checking off final components + big ideas	- summary collaboration
	Ava	- summary - fast facts		

Figure 5.14

Students successfully worked through independent inquiry projects, so we wanted to extend their opportunity for responding to informational texts. We told students they would be co-researching for their next inquiry project related to space. The class cheered. We presented the co-researching anchor chart in Figure 5.13. We explained, "Co-researching isn't just two people reading separate books and putting all their information together at the end. A partnership includes reading, discussing, and documenting before, during, and after reading. You will be turning in only one inquiry folder together on Fridays." We explained that we would be using a different format for this project, a lapbook instead of a poster. We gave them details of the requirements and showed them a model including informational writing, temperature and weather, surface and atmosphere, number of moons, fast facts, image or diagram, and an interactive Wow pop-up (a paper folded in half labeled that can be lifted up to read interesting/Wow facts). More information about lapbooks can be found at https://lapbooking.wordpress.com/lapbook/. We selected a specific format for the final product to increase students' collaborative independence. By reducing the options for their final product, they only had to co-research and negotiate how to complete it with their partners.

"You can bring additional information that you learn on your own to your co-researching sessions, but you have to decide together the most important learning to include in your weekly response and final project." This sometimes sparked debate or questions because students would find slightly different information about their same topic from different sources. This was exactly the kind of thinking, negotiating, and discussing we hoped would happen. We used the note-taking guide to conduct quick observations and confer with research teams/partners as needed. We also provided weekly feedback on their collaborative reading response submission of their inquiry folders/lapbooks on Fridays.

The co-researchers presented their self-selected topic to the rest of the class. Then, students worked together to create a mural that represented their understanding of space and the planets based on their collaborative research. This mural and their lapbooks were displayed in the hallway for other students and parents to view. The students did an amazing job with the lapbooks and mural as seen in Figure 5.15 and Figure 5.16.

In the following weeks and units, students chose their own topics and presentation formats for co-researching inquiry projects. These alternative formats and possibilities for collaboration deepened the engagement and motivation to respond to informational texts.

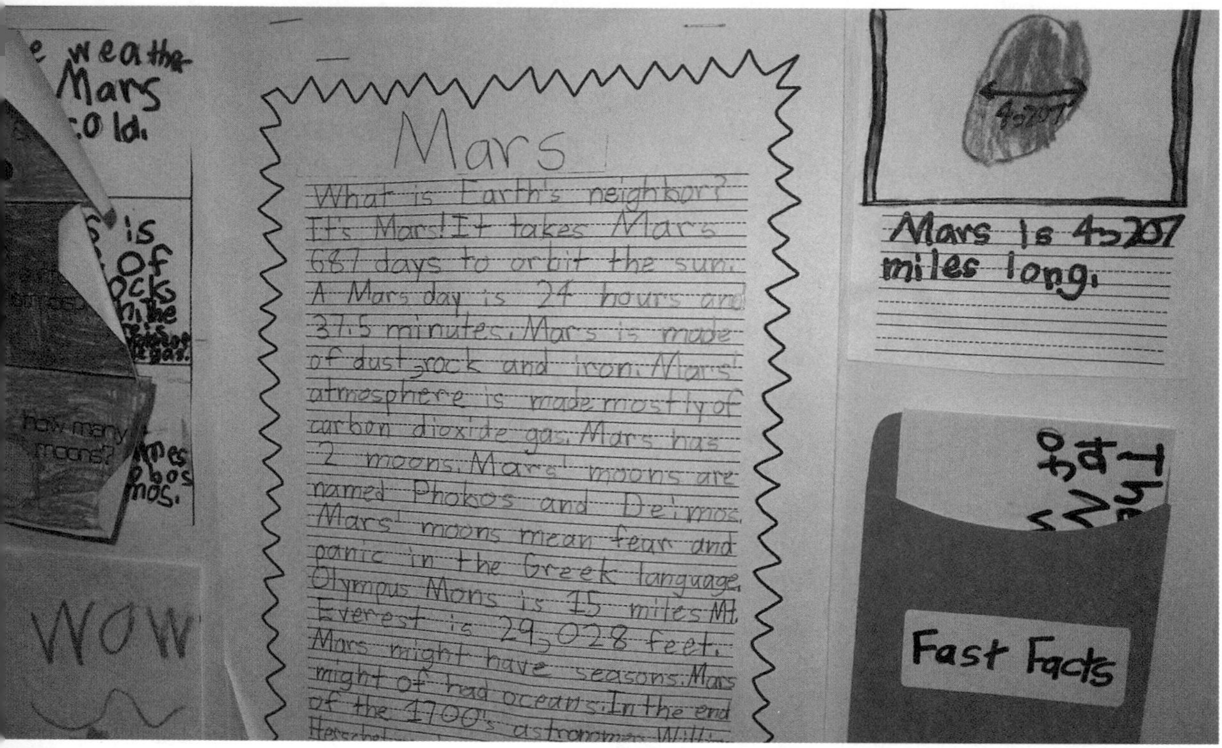

Figure 5.15 Alexis' lapbook made her research interactive. She had pop-ups with information inside and note cards that students could take out that included "fast facts."

Figure 5.16 Students took their big thinking to create a big mural of the planets.

EXTENDING

1. Review the option for inspired writing for narrative texts.

2. Create an "Author's Craft" chart for a favorite informational author.

3. Explain that writing using an author's craft shows a deep understanding of the author's words as well as the application of students' own thinking and ideas.

4. Introduce writing informational texts as a new option for postreading response on Fridays.

5. Provide opportunities for sharing, feedback, and publishing.

Peek into Our Classroom

The students completed some outstanding inquiry projects. However, we felt we could deepen the learning by providing a more authentic audience and format with inspired writing for informational texts. We had an upcoming author visit from Frank Serafini, so students had been reading his Looking Closely series. We said, "Informational author's craft is just as important as fiction, but it is often very different. Let's brainstorm ideas from Frank Serafini's books." Students brainstormed ideas as we created the anchor chart in Figure 5.17.

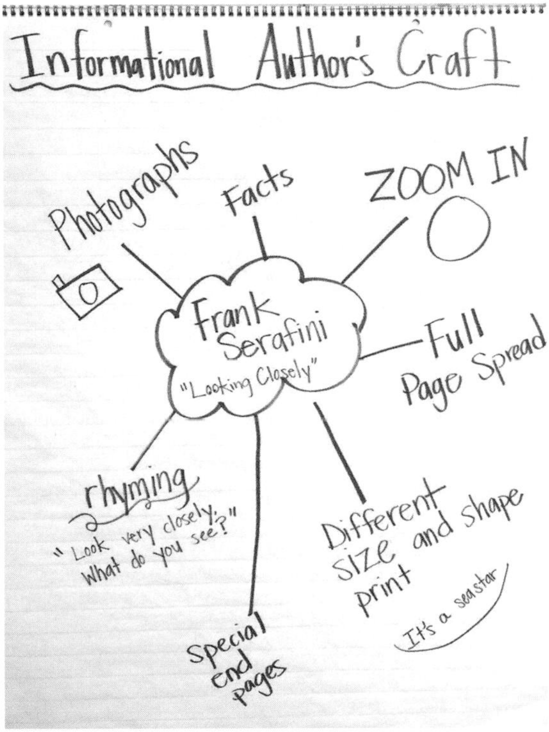

Diego: He always zooms in really close on the first picture.

Aubri: Rhyming words. He always uses rhyming words on those pages.

Evelynn: Facts. The facts are in a paragraph on the page with the big picture.

Teachers: A lot of you are talking about the photographs. What about the photographs as part of his craft?

Shaun: The pictures are the best part of his author's craft!

Sophia: He fills the Os in with a picture on the cover. He makes the words look different, like big, small, dark.

Sam: He also has pictures in the endpages.

Figure 5.17 "Informational Author's Craft" anchor chart

We asked students to generate questions for the author as seen in Figure 5.18. During Frank Serafini's presentation, he talked about his process and craft as both the author and illustrator. He emphasized the importance of photography, research, writing, and revision. The students were captivated and had a chance to try on his equipment and discuss what it's like to be an author. As you can imagine, this sparked extensive informational writing inspired by the Looking Closely series.

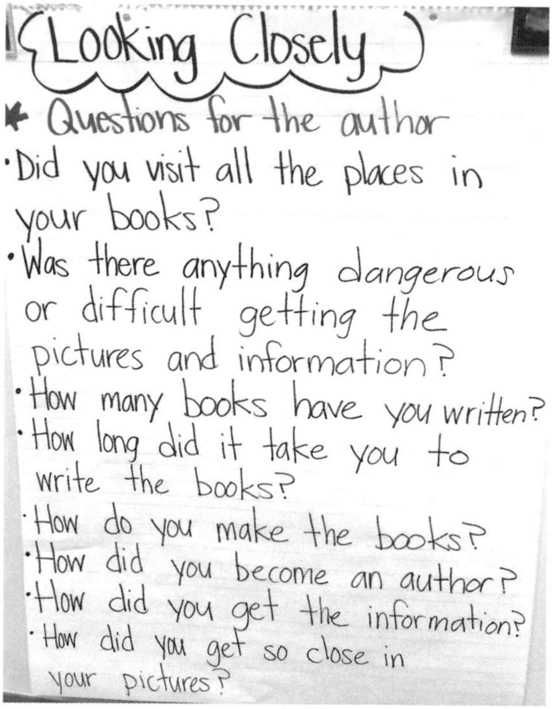

Looking Closely

→ Questions for the author

- Did you visit all the places in your books?
- Was there anything dangerous or difficult getting the pictures and information?
- How many books have you written?
- How long did it take you to write the books?
- How do you make the books?
- How did you become an author?
- How did you get the information?
- How did you get so close in your pictures?

Figure 5.18 The students generated more than three poster pages of questions for the author.

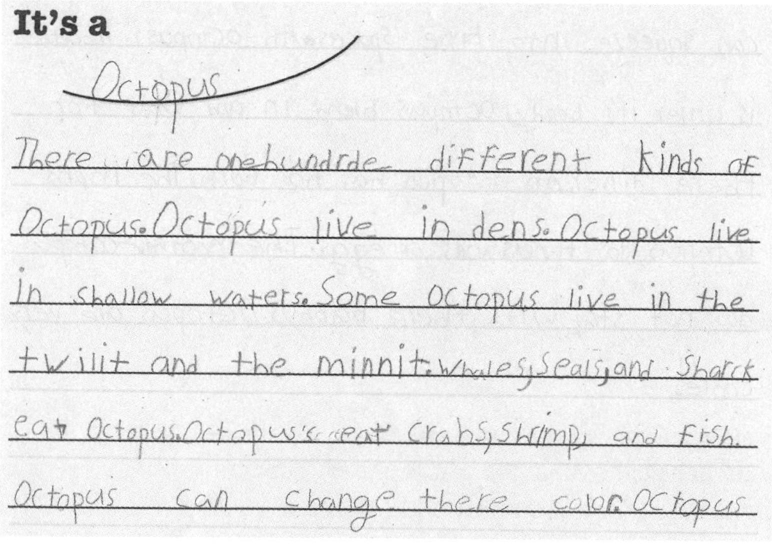

It's a

Octopus

There are onehundrde different kinds of Octopus. Octopus live in dens. Octopus live in shallow waters. Some octopus live in the twilit and the minnit. Whales, Seals, and Sharck eat Octopus. Octopus's eat Crabs, Shrimp, and fish. Octopus can change there color. Octopus

Figure 5.19 Lacie's writing, inspired by the Looking Closely series

Everyone wanted to write a piece inspired by the Looking Closely series, so we discussed the essential components from the author's craft. Then, we created a common outline so students could make their own books or contribute to a class book. Lacie added to the essential components of "Look very closely. What do you see?" with questions and guesses that resembled the close-up of the image she selected followed by the informational paragraph (Figure 5.19). Students placed their informational writing in their reading response journal for the Friday submissions. Students had opportunities to share their inspired informational writing during partner reading and small groups. If they decided to continue work on the writing and publish it, it became part of our classroom library of books authored by students, or they could keep it in their reading box. The inquiry and inspired reading responses gave students opportunities to think deeper, collaborate, and share research with an audience of their peers. The publications and presentation formats facilitated discussion and engagement about their thinking. This gave students independence and choice in how they documented their meaning making with informational texts.

ASSESSING PROGRESS

Our note-taking guides evolved throughout the year as we refined our expectations for inquiry reading responses and projects. We also created and revised rubrics and inquiry checklists that were shared with students. Students used these as guidelines and checklists. We used them to provide weekly feedback when they submitted their inquiry folders. These assessments shaped conferring, minilessons, and small-group sessions with students. Throughout the year, routines would break down or need revisiting, and note-taking guides and rubrics quickly documented those needs.

Considerations in kindergarten and second grade

	Teacher Modifications	Student Expectations
K	· Create adapted text for informational topics of interest. · Provide videos and/or audiobooks on topics of interest. · Reduce number of required nonfiction text features for posters. · Allow for more images and oral presentations (with scribing as appropriate). · Modify lapbook (eliminate summary/report, add more visuals, decrease number of fast facts). · Support small-group researching.	· Need assistance reading informational texts. · Demonstrate understanding with images, labels, and captions. · Use oral language and visuals to demonstrate and present new learning and understanding. · Co-research in small group with teacher support.
2	· Provide access to additional technology and research options. · Extend independent inquiry options beyond common topics/themes. · Present many different inquiry project formats (TED talks, wikis, models, and so on). · Extend expectations for research and documentation (citing sources, extended writing and information, additional nonfiction text features).	· Read more complex text with a variety of text-based and online sources. · Demonstrate understanding with five or more nonfiction text features. · Use visual, written, and oral language to document and share research. · Collaborate with peers to conduct research and present findings with classmates and/or other students and adults. · Connect individual research to broader topics and issues.

Calendar

	Week 1	Week 2	Week 3	Week 4	Week 5	Week 6	Week 7–Dec.	Jan.	Feb.–June
Introduce "I learned" and "I wonder" sticky notes						X			
Introduce nonfiction text features to support future inquiry						X	X	X	X
Independent inquiry projects								X	X
Collaborative inquiry projects									X
Self-selected inquiry projects									X
Confer with research groups and individuals								X	X

6 · Partner Experiences that Foster Collaborative Independence

It's mid-September and we're finally settling into our routines. The children quickly pair up, choose a spot, and agree upon a book to read. At first glance everything looks great. Students are sitting side by side, the book is in the middle, and they appear to be reading. As we listen into different partnerships, we realize not everyone is as productive and independent as we thought.

Emily and Wyatt are taking turns reading, but as Emily reads Wyatt gazes off, leaving her unsupported and mumbling through unknown words. She gently taps him to let him know it's his turn. He quickly and accurately reads his page, and then it is back to Emily. They continue reading the book, never truly interacting with each other. This is independently reading next to a friend, not partner reading.

Ramone and Alex are engaged in an informational book. They are pointing and sharing their background knowledge about each animal on the page. But as they read on, Ramone becomes fully engrossed in the book, so much so that he has completely moved the book onto his lap, excluding Alex from the partner reading experience. Here we recognize the importance of maintaining stamina with a partner.

Aubree and Samantha are taking turns, actively attending to text, and paying attention to one another. Samantha pauses for a moment, thinking about a word. Before she has time to apply her strategies, Aubree swoops in and tells her the word. This happens several times over the next few pages. Although this pair is on task and both partners are involved, we question whether the partners are encouraging each other to grow as readers.

Finally, we make our way to Aubri and Farah. They are both kneeling over a Mo Willems book and appear to be actively engaged. Aubri is tracking the print and using an expressive voice while she reads and Farah looks on. Aubri gets stuck on a word and says, "I don't know this word." Farah looks closely at the word and replies, "Look at the beginning sound. It starts with a p. What would make sense?" Aubri tries, but produces a word that does not make sense. Farah prompts her again, "It has a bossy r so you can't really hear the e." With a gasp of excitement, Aubri blurts out the word, personal. They continue reading, laughing, and supporting one another throughout the book. This partner reading experience feels like a victory and one that must be shared with the class.

🐦 🐦 🐦

I n this chapter, we discuss collaborative independence, where students work successfully with partners without the direct support of the teacher. We focus on two
distinct opportunities for literacy-related partner experiences: coaching and talking.
The initial stages of fostering collaborative independence are noisy, but don't let that scare
you away. Expect the noise, excitement, and challenges before the students settle into
comfortable, meaningful, and quieter interactions without you. Like all
aspects of fostering independence in the primary grades, it takes
various stages of support and continuous revisiting to maintain
and deepen their experiences engaging with
texts and other children.

Questions primary teachers ask
about fostering collab-
orative indepen-
dence include the
following:

- How can young readers support one another when reading?
- Will being with a partner distract them from reading?
- How can readers who are struggling to decode text "coach" or "talk"?
- Will one student dominate the reading, coaching, and talking?
- How do we know the students are using the time as intended?
- How do you choose partners?

These questions arose out of challenges we encountered during different attempts at partner reading experiences. We were challenged with making thoughtful partnerships; some worked well and others did not. We loved the idea of students supporting each other by asking if their partner needed time or coaching (Boushey and Moser 2014), but we were disappointed with the way this actually played out in our classroom. Finally, it was extremely challenging to get children moving beyond literal and low-level conversations about the books they were reading. Solving these challenges wasn't easy and was constantly a work in progress, but partners were independently coaching and discussing texts in thoughtful ways by midyear.

Supporting Research: Why Is It Important? Does It Really Work?

Partner reading is important for many reasons. Literacy is a socially constructed activity involving reading, writing, speaking, listening, viewing, and visually representing. Reading together and talking about books can provide partners with enriching experiences, thinking, and conversation that would not take place while reading independently. In addition to the motivation, engagement, and social aspects, Rogoff (1990) documented interactions between partners that led to each child achieving a higher level of understanding than working by themselves. This could be due to the type of talk surrounding partner reading. Brown (2006) found five major themes of talk occurred during partner reading time in second grade: organizational, disputational, word strategy, meaning making, and personal talk. All of these, except personal talk, supported partner reading.

Partner selection and instructional support influence talk and success in partner reading. Meisinger and colleagues (2004) found that students who chose their own partner were more successful with social cooperation (instrumental support, emotional support, and conflict management) than when the partner was chosen by the teacher. However, if neither child had the skills to support the reading and/or no one needed support, their time off task increased. The authors also recommended avoiding similar-ability partnerships. This was supported by other research suggesting partnering students of moderately different abilities was ideal (Rogoff 1990; Topping

1989). However, other research and books recommend partnering students at the same reading level (Calkins 2000; Collins 2004; Griffin 2002).

In addition to reading abilities, choice, and personality, instruction related to interactions, coaching, and conversations plays an important role in the success of partner reading experiences. Students have stronger instrumental support, emotional support, and conflict management (social cooperation) when teachers provide basic support or scripts for coaching and partner interactions in the beginning of the year. Students who receive elaborate or no instruction are associated with poorer social cooperation (Meisinger et al. 2004). This research helped us understand that students needed modeling and continued support on deepening their interactions with partners and texts, but too much scripting or instruction might stifle their opportunities for flexible talk.

Partner Coaching

Because the research on ideal partner pairings was mixed (Rogoff 1990; Topping 1989 vs. Calkins 2000; Collins 2004; Griffin 2002), we created multiple partnerships throughout the year: same ability level, slightly different levels, and choice partners. There were periods of only one type of partnership and other periods where we altered partners (A partners, B partners, and so on) depending on our goals for partner reading that day. In full disclosure, we also made some partner decisions based primarily on personality and behavior. With these students, we took their literacy abilities into account, but personality sometimes took priority.

We wanted to maximize the benefit of partner reading by encouraging students to support each other in the reading process. This involved responsive opportunities to give prompts and suggestions to assist partners when they encountered difficult words. We hoped to avoid students simply reading the word for their partner. Instead, we promoted shared responsibility in coaching using strategies that were introduced to the whole group (these are explained in greater depth in Chapter 4).

PREASSESSING

1. Assign partners at approximately the same reading level.
2. Have students find a space and read with a partner for ten minutes.
3. Observe and take notes about reading behaviors (What are they doing? Who is reading? How are they positioned? How do they take turns? Whose books

are they reading? What do they do when they get stuck on a word?) See the observational guide in Figure 6.1.

4. Bring them together and discuss their partner reading experience.

5. Use questions from the observations to expand and document conversation, as seen in Figure 6.2.

Peek into Our Classroom

We assigned partners who were reading at approximately the same level, based on our observations and Developmental Reading Assessment scores. We asked them to find a "good spot," like they did during independent reading, to read with their partner for ten minutes. We used the open-ended observational note-taking guide seen in Figure 6.1 to document observations.

Partner Reading Open Ended Note-Taking Guide

	What are they doing?	Who is reading?	How are they positioned?	How do they take turns?	Whose book are they reading?	What do they do when they get stuck on a word?
LM OW	LM reading whole book	LM	side by side	don't	LM	Not observed (NO)
CF RL	flipping pages	neither	side by side	random	RL	(NO)
FS MO	choral reading	both	side by side	—	FS	- pause + both try
SG CW	Unrelated talking	(NO)	face to face	—	—	—
SW WC	taking turns reading	both	side by side	by pages	SW	SW tells WC
CL JM	both reading their own books	both	near each other	don't	own	asks partner
TM MS	taking turns reading	both	side by side	by character	MS	looks at pic.

Figure 6.1 Partner Reading Open-Ended Note-Taking Guide

Children loudly negotiated where they were going to sit. Some partnerships sat very near other partnerships, but we didn't say anything because we wanted to see how they would work it out. Some children appeared eager to read with their partners. However, once they found their spots (the first time it took nearly five minutes for all students to get seated), we saw a wide range of partner interactions. Here are some of the behaviors we observed:

- arguing over what book to read or who was going to read first
- some students seated next to each other and others sitting face-to-face
- individuals reading their own books
- one student reading while the other student looked on
- unrelated talking to their partner or other partner groups
- getting up and moving around the room
- flipping through books
- choral reading
- taking turns reading
- talking about the book.

We called the students together to debrief their first partner reading experience. We asked students the open-ended question, "How did partner reading go?" The students responded with mixed reports ranging from "Great!" to "Bad, my partner was talking and goofing off the entire time." After students shared their experiences, we reported our observations. We asked students to chat with their partner about one thing that went well and one thing that might need to change. Then, we created an anchor chart about partner reading experiences seen in Figure 6.2.

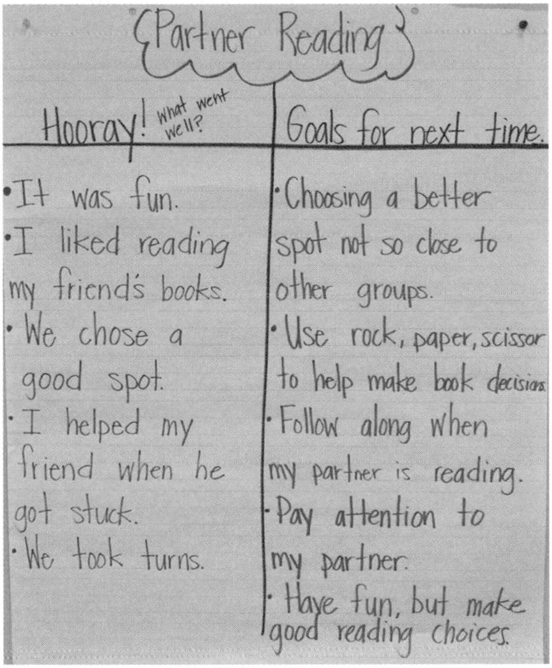

Figure 6.2 Students shared success and goals for partner reading. Their experiences and goals became the expectations for partner reading.

TEACHING

1. Revisit the T-chart from the first partner reading.
2. Ask students to help create class expectations on an anchor chart. Discuss the purpose of partner reading and the basic requirements such as expectations, turn

taking, physical positioning (elbow to elbow, knee to knee) (Boushey and Moser 2014), and so on, as seen in Figure 6.3.

3. Start a partner coaching anchor chart similar to Figure 6.4. Explain that readers typically benefit from three types of partner support: time, coaching, or reading the word.

4. Model getting stuck on a word and then solving it. Explain that sometimes readers need extra time to use their strategies before they figure out a word, so it is helpful if partners wait quietly for a few seconds.

5. Ask students to silently count to three before asking if you need more time or if you want coaching.

6. Interactively model the process with students.

7. Tell them you need coaching, and ask students to turn and talk about what clues or strategies they think might help you. Refer back to the strategies chart in Figure 4.1. (See the example in Chapter 4.)

8. Use student suggestions to model applying a strategy to figure out the word.

9. Tell students to suggest two clues/strategies before reading the word to their partner.

Partner Reading

♥ Building Independence Together ♥

Why: To become better readers and thinkers together. To have FUN!

1. Stay in your book - reading and thinking together
2. Use soft voices
3. Choose a just right spot for two
4. Stay in one spot
5. Sit EEKK
6. Get started right away
7. You read... I read
8. Retell, discuss book, ask questions
9. Have fun reading!

Figure 6.3 "Partner Reading" anchor chart with purpose and procedures. Adapted from Boushey and Moser (2014).

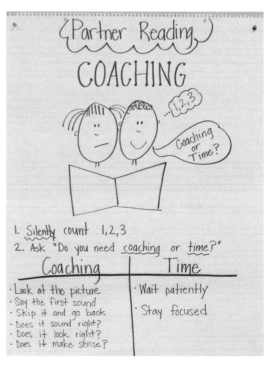

1. Silently count 1,2,3
2. Ask "Do you need coaching or time?"

Coaching	Time
· Look at the picture	· Wait patiently
· Say the first sound	· Stay focused
· Skip it and go back	
· Does it sound right?	
· Does it look right?	
· Does it make sense?	

Figure 6.4 The "Partner Reading: Coaching" anchor chart includes visuals and specific examples.

We created an anchor chart with the title "Partner Reading: Building Independence Together" and our purposes for partner reading, "To become better readers and thinkers. To have fun!" We placed this chart next to the initial chart we created (Figure 6.2) about students' successes and challenges of partner reading. The students immediately generated and shared ideas about what should happen during partner reading based on their previous experiences. Saige said, "Read the whole time." Aubree added, "Stay in your spot and don't be too loud." Dax said, "Take turns," and Diego said, "Who gets to go first?" We decided on one Rock, Paper, Scissors contest to decide the first book choice and first page of reading. They were very focused on the behavior and procedural components (numbers one through seven in Figure 6.3). We appreciated their attention to expectations, but also wanted to emphasize the importance of reading for meaning and enjoyment. We suggested and added (with their permission) numbers eight and nine.

We told students one benefit of reading with a partner is they can help you when you get stuck on a word. We said, "Sometimes when I am reading and come to a word I don't know, I just need a little more time to figure it out. It makes me feel frustrated when someone just shouts out the word because I know I could've figured it out on my own." We asked students to raise a thumb if they had experienced this, and almost all of them did. We explained partners could help in three ways: (1) time, (2) coaching, (3) reading the word. We showed them the partner coaching anchor chart in Figure 6.4.

We modeled reading a big book aloud and getting stuck on a word. We told students to silently count to three, and then ask us, "Do you need time or coaching?" First, we said, "Time," and modeled figuring out the word on our own. Then, we practiced getting stuck again. Students silently counted to three and asked us if we needed coaching or time. We told them we needed help. We asked them to talk to a partner about a clue or fix-up strategy that might help us figure out the word. Students shared their suggestions, and we modeled using them to figure out the word. We went back and reread the sentence again. Finally, we explained that sometimes, even with coaching, we could not figure out the word. We told them to read the word to their partner if they had tried two strategies without success.

SCAFFOLDING

1. Review the "Partner Reading: Coaching" chart.
2. Model partner reading and coaching with a student.
3. Begin partner reading and observe using the observational guide in Figure 6.1.
4. Confer with partners.

5. Debrief with students about partner reading and coaching.

6. Continue partner reading opportunities and observations with additional conferring and support as needed.

We placed the anchor charts side by side and chorally read them as a class. We invited Owen to sit beside Meridith and model the coaching options. When she paused on a word, he counted to three on his fingers and then politely asked, "Do you want more time or do you want help?" She told him she needed time and then sounded the word out and reread the sentence. After pausing on another word, Owen asked her if she needed time or help. She asked for help. His first suggestion was to tap out each sound. The word was *thick*, so when she tried that strategy, she said two separate sounds /t/ /h/ for *th*. Owen looked puzzled at first, but then suggested she try to chunk it and check to see what would make sense. This strategy worked. We used this opportunity to have a quick conversation about how some strategies work for some words, but not for others. Owen said, "I should've used chunking first. Tapping didn't work with *thick*." We talked about what great thinking he did to figure out clues to help Meridith, but also matched the strategy with the word and problem she was having. We told students to try this as they worked with their partners.

The initial observations were mixed. Some students were very diligent in following the expectations and protocol, but others talked, laughed, argued, read independently, and/or just read the word when their partner got stuck. We completed the observational guide and conferred with students who needed redirection and additional support. At this point, less than half the class was doing what we had hoped would happen in partner reading and coaching. We debriefed with students about what went well and what needed work. As they shared their reflections and we shared our observations, we noted they were very similar to our initial reflections about partner reading. This initial collaboration took longer than we originally anticipated. The students were excited, and the focus and concentration was a challenge for some students. Over two weeks, we changed some partnerships based on personalities, and we continued revisiting expectations, conferring, and supporting during partner reading. This meant no small-group time, but it was well worth it once they were able to read and coach in quiet and meaningful ways with their partners.

MONITORING AND REFINING

1. After providing additional support and conferring until students are independent, begin meeting with small groups during this time.

2. Use the Partner Reading 90 Seconds Observational Checklist in Figure 6.5 (a blank template is included in the appendices) for observations. Use

Partner Reading 90 Seconds Observational Checklist

	Choral reading	Taking turns	One reading	Silent	Both see book	2 different	Equal	One dominating	Transition	Rock, paper	Related talk	Unrelated talk	One off task	Both off-task	Coaching- Time	Coaching- Fix
LM OW		ı			ı		ı									ı
CF RL			ı										ı			
FS MO						ı										
SG CS		ı					ı									
SW WC	ı				ı		ı					ı				
CL JM									ı	ı						
TM MS		ı						ı								ı
SR JE												ı		ı		
ER WL		ı			ı		ı				ı					
MN AB		ı			ı		ı									
DG CR												ı		ı		
BB KL		ı			ı			ı								
AK AS				ı		ı										
LB ZB			ı											ı		

Figure 6.5 Partner Reading 90 Seconds Observational Checklist

daily initially, but then shift to weekly check-ins as students become more independent.

3. Provide specific coaching strategies on a sticky note from conferring or small group, as needed.

4. Periodically meet with the class to reflect on coaching strategies students use frequently (as a reader and coach).

5. Create new partnerships (try self-selected, same-ability, and mixed-ability partnerships).

6. Give the partnerships names (A partners, B partners, and so on) to allow for quick transitions when changing partnerships.

It took over two weeks for our students to become independent in partner reading and coaching and we could pull small groups. We explained we were unavailable during this time so students could revisit the anchor charts or work with a partner to solve problems (the same expectations as independent reading). During the first week with no conferring or support during partner reading, we used a quick checklist at the middle and end of partner reading. We created this checklist based on our initial observations, and it took us about ninety seconds to complete using tallies. This helped us assess students' time on task and if and when we needed to provide support. After the first week, we did one checklist a week and briefly shared information with students after partner reading. Some students were still struggling to provide appropriate coaching suggestions to their partner. We met with the partnerships and gave them targeted coaching prompts on a sticky note that they could use during independent reading and their partner could use when coaching.

The expectations and routines became an automatic daily experience for students. We kept the partners together for three to six weeks because we wanted them to get to know each other as readers. In addition to applying effective coaching strategies, they recommended and selected books for each other. To maintain their growth from partner reading and begin building metacognition, we asked students to reflect on the following three things with their partner: What strategy do they use the most when they get stuck on a word? What strategy does their partner recommend that is usually the most helpful for them? What strategy do they recommend that is most helpful for their partner? These discussions, as seen in the introductory vignette, provided opportunities for students to thoughtfully reflect on their experiences as a reader and a partner.

Throughout the year, we changed partnerships so students would have partners with similar and mixed reading abilities. We also let students self-select partners. We called these partners different names so we could switch partners depending on our goals for that day or week.

EXTENDING

1. Review the fix-up strategies students have been using during coaching experiences.

2. Explain that coaching should include fix-up and strategies to read with expression.

3. Review the anchor charts about reading with expression like the one seen in Figure 6.6.

4. Model reading with a partner, providing a fix-up strategy, and coaching to read with expression.

5. Ask students to try coaching to read with expression during partner reading.

6. Debrief and reflect on the coaching points they used the most.

7. Add prosody elements/coaching to your observational checklist. (See Figure 6.7.)

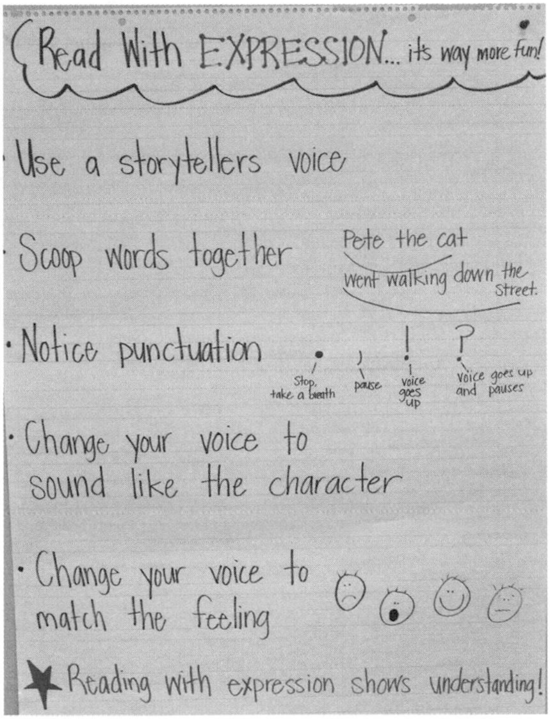

Peek into Our Classroom

We read the initial pages of *A Big Guy Took My Ball!* (Willems 2013) aloud as quickly as possible in a monotone voice that didn't change for characters or pause for punctuation. Jonathan quickly said, "Come on, read it right." We had previously talked about the importance of adhering to punctuation and reading with expression, so we pulled out those anchor charts to remind students about how to read with expression. The students loved Mo Willems, and we thought his books provided great opportunities to support and scaffold a focus on expression.

Figure 6.6 "Read with Expression" anchor chart

We quickly reviewed the charts and discussed the importance of looking for clues the author and illustrator gave us, showing punctuation, typography, and speech bubble examples. We discussed the importance of paying attention to this because it changed how readers experienced the story. We told students we noticed reading with expression was missing for many students during partner reading, so we were adding this to our coaching options.

We modeled partner reading with *A Big Guy Took My Ball!* (Willems 2013) again. Prior to reading, we had the following conversation:

Meridith: In most books, we just take turns for each page, but I think it might make sense for us to take turns for characters. It would make our reading with expression better, don't you think?

Lindsey: Yes, Mo Willems gives different colors for the voices in speech bubbles to match each character in the Elephant and Piggie books. Can I be Gerald?

Meridith: Sure, I will be Piggie. Remember, we are going to be coaching for words, but also for reading with expression.

	Choral reading	Taking turns	One reading	Silent	Both see book	2 different books	Equal relationships	One dominating	Transition	Rock, paper, scissors	Related talk	Unrelated talk	One off task	Both off-task	Coaching- Time	Coaching- Fix Up Strat	Coaching- Expression
LM OW		|			|		|									S	
CF RL		|						|									
FS MO			|									|					
SG CS		|			|		|				|						S
SW WC									|	|	~						
CL JM		|					|										N
TM MS		|			|		|										
SR JE		|			|			|								S	
ER WL												|					
MN AB		|			|		|				|						
DG CR		|						|			|		.			S	N
BB KL													|				
AK AS		|			|		|					|				S	
LB ZB	|				|												

S= Successfully Coaching

N= Needs Support

Figure 6.7

Meridith began reading. When she didn't change her intonation or volume level for the word *Gerald* in a bold, large font followed by an exclamation mark, I said, "Could you reread that page and use the chart clues to read with expression?" Meridith reread the page, and we continued modeling for three more pages. We modeled coaching for time, fix-up strategy, and reading with expression because we wanted to emphasize that we were coaching for all three options.

Students practiced with their partners. This brought a renewed excitement to partner reading. Students became more engaged in the process and paid closer attention to the design elements, font, punctuation, and performance aspects of reading aloud. Evelynn said to her partner, "Can you reread that page? I think Gerald is supposed to sound scared—look at the movement marks, like he is shaking and scared."

We debriefed about their new coaching experiences. Many students used books by Mo Willems on the first day, so they talked about reading like different characters. One student said, "It was really funny when we read like that today. It was kinda like we're getting ready to be in a movie." We asked for other volunteers who did not read Mo Willems to share their experiences about coaching with expression. Aubree said, "Well, we had to create another voice. A voice for when no one was speaking. The one that was just the book telling what was going on. So we made that sound different than when people were talking." We briefly talked about the role of a narrator, and then asked students to keep this in mind during their reading and partner coaching.

ASSESSING

Our behavior checklists and observations evolved throughout the year. Observation guided the instruction and support we provided to help students develop collaborative independence to read and support each other in partners. Observations were initially related to what students were doing during partner reading and became more sophisticated as we introduced coaching strategies related to time, fix-up, and reading with expression. Our assessments moved to quick ninety-second observational checklists. See Figure 6.7 for our final version of the checklist related to coaching. For the coaching columns, we use a coding scheme instead of tallies. If students successfully coached, we marked it with an *S*. If students attempted coaching but needed additional support, we coded it as *N*. We left it blank if there was no attempt. This helped guide our revisiting, conferring, and discussions about coaching.

Students' conversations and reflections about coaching helped them develop metacognition about how they were reading and strategies they could use to support their own reading in other contexts. This provided opportunities for self-assessment so students could take ownership of the reading, coaching, and partnership experiences.

Considerations in kindergarten and second grade

	Teacher Modifications	Student Expectations
K	· Shorten times for partner reading (15 minutes might be the maximum amount of time). · Provide a greater emphasis on multiple options for approximated reading (pictures, design features, retelling, and reading the words). · Simplify coaching options to two or three focus fix-up strategies with the option for skipping or guessing after two attempts. · Provide additional support with text selection and initial coaching strategies through conferring and extra support in the initial stages.	· Use approximated reading to participate in partner reading. · Develop partner reading stamina up to 15 minutes. · Can use two or three fix-up strategies when coaching their partner.
2	· Extend partner reading time to 20–30 minutes. · Ask students to collaboratively select some texts for partner reading because they will be reading longer texts over multiple sessions. · Provide less instructional focus on fix-up strategies and greater focus on thoughtful coaching recommendations based on the specific text challenges. · Introduce the expression *coaching* during the first week of partner experiences.	· Participate in longer periods of reading complex texts that carry over multiple partner reading periods. · Identify specific and appropriate coaching prompts. · Need less focus on fix-up strategies, but may need additional support with expression.

Calendar

	Week 1	Week 2	Week 3	Week 4	Week 5	Week 6	Week 7–Dec.	Jan.	Feb.–June
Partner assignments (change every 3–6 weeks on a per needs basis)				X			X	X	X
Open-ended note taking				X					
Observational checklist				X	X	X	X	X	X
Partner reflections				X	X	X	X	X	X
Introduce building independence together				X	X				
Introduce coaching					X				
Introduce partner strategy instruction					X	X			
Introduce reading with expression							X	X	X
Needs-based small groups					X	X	X	X	X
Partner conferring				X	X	X	X	X	X

William wiggles onto our book talk stool, straightens up, looks out at his audience, takes a deep breath, and begins to tell his friends all about his favorite book for the week, Duck on a Bike *(Shannon 2002). "If you thought* No David *was funny, wait until you read* Duck on a Bike." *William knows how to hook his audience. He makes a text-to-text connection, recognizes the author's craft of humor, and draws upon his knowledge of his peers. He concludes his book talk with, "I suggest you read this book to find out Duck's wild idea. It's sure to make you laugh." Hands immediately fly into the air. The children want to know which basket you could find it in and if we had more than one copy. William sits on the stool grinning ear to ear, knowing he just sold his book. From then on, it was all about pitching a good book. Could students convince their friends their favorite book for the week was worth reading too?*

Book talks spark conversations and heighten students' awareness about the types of books available in our classroom library. They don't take more than a few minutes, but they teach the children how to start talking about books in an engaging and meaningful way. Book talks are a small step toward grander conversations. They show the value of talking about books, but most importantly, when done well, they have the power to inspire other readers.

🐾 🐾 🐾

Partner Talk

Conversations about text lead to increased motivation and engagement and a higher level of understanding than working independently (Rogoff 1990). We felt challenged by the initial lack of conversation initiative and depth, even when prompted to discuss the books. Partner coaching was successful, and we encouraged students to talk about their books, but it was clear they needed more structure and support to engage in conversations about meaning making and interpretive responses.

PREASSESSMENT

1. Observe your students during partner reading.

2. Prompt students to talk about a book during and after reading.

3. Document the type of talking and interactions that take place during and after reading (see the note-taking guide in Figure 6.8; a blank template is included in the appendices).

Peek into Our Classroom

Partner reading with coaching was going well, but we wanted to deepen students' partner experiences with engaging conversation. We reminded students they could and should be talking about their thinking when reading books with partners. Then, we observed.

Even with the specific reminder about discussion, most students only talked about coaching elements. No one talked about meaning making or impressions during

Partner Reading: Talk Note-Taking Guide

	What are they talking about during reading?	Discussion after reading
LM OW	coaching prompts	liked book
CF RL	nothing	liked book
FS MO	nothing	choosing next book
SG CS	arguing about turn	liked book
SW WC	making a connection	unrelated talking.
CL JM	laughing	thought book was funny

Figure 6.8

the reading. Four partners talked about the book after reading it. The following are samples of what we heard:

- "I liked that book." "Me too."
- "We need to talk about the book." "I thought it was funny."
- "I learned all kinds of stuff about sharks." "Mmhm, I get to pick the next book."
- "That book was really easy for me."

We were glad the students had positive things to say and seemed to enjoy their reading, but it was evident we needed to provide additional support for getting started with partner conversations.

TEACHING

1. Share observations about partner conversation.
2. Explain that readers recommend and discuss books. Present anchor charts with two options for talking about books after reading (see Figures 6.9, 6.10).
3. Model retelling and a book talk about a familiar book.

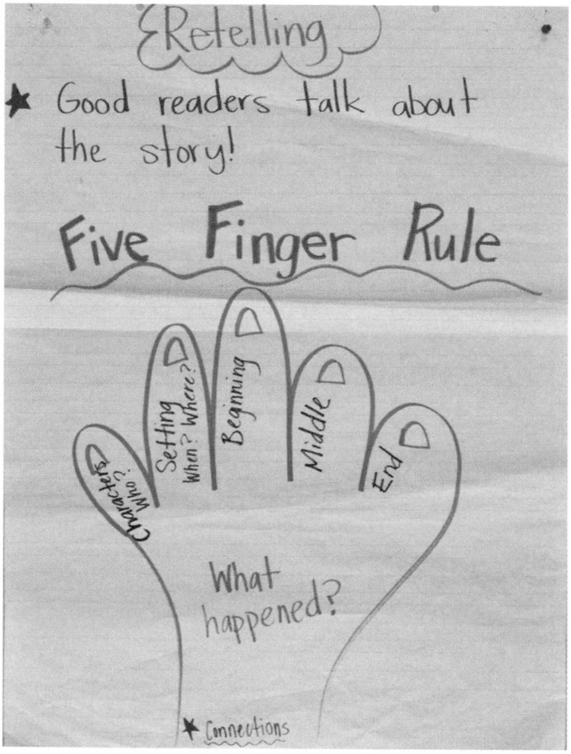

Figure 6.9 We created the five finger retell anchor chart with purpose and procedures. The students added a bracelet for making connections.

Figure 6.10 The "Book Talks" anchor chart includes language frames, transition words, and the purpose for sharing.

We told students we noticed them doing a great job with their partner coaching, and we heard many students talking about whether or not they liked the book they were reading. We explained that good readers talk about what happened in books they read and recommend books to friends. We displayed two anchor charts and told students they would have a choice of responding using either of the formats: book talk or retelling.

Students were familiar with the five finger retell because it was a comprehension check strategy we introduced previously. Book talks were new. We explained that when one of us reads a new book, we share it with the other by telling a little bit about the book and recommending whether or not the other should read it. We told students they would be using book talks for two purposes. The first was to think, talk, and reflect on the book they read with their partner. The second was to share the book talk they practiced with their partner with a small group on Fridays prior to book shopping. We wanted students to debrief about their reading in ways that were deeper than "I like the book" during partner reading, but we also wanted them to understand the authentic purposes of book talks: to share with friends your thinking and recommendations.

We modeled a structured book talk about a book we were reading that week, *Wemberly Worried* (Henkes 2000). Following the anchor chart seen in Figure 6.10, we said, "I read *Wemberly Worried* by Kevin Henkes. First, Wemberly was so worried about everything, especially going to school. Next, she went to school and the kids teased her. Then, she made a friend and things began to change. I would recommend this book because it is a little funny and reminded me not to worry so much. Questions, comments, connections?" Students responded to our model book talk by making connections to times when they worried and telling us about other Kevin Henkes' books they have read. We talked about how important and fun it is to talk about books because it helps us understand them better and think deeper.

SCAFFOLDING

1. Review the "Retelling" and "Book Talks" anchor charts.
2. Ask students to begin partner reading and include a retell or book talk at the end of each book.
3. Observe partner talk using the note-taking guide in Figure 6.11 (a blank template is included in the appendices).
4. Confer with partners.
5. Ask students to debrief about partner reading and talk.
6. Continue partner reading opportunities and observations.
7. Provide additional support as needed with conferring.

Partner Reading: Conversing Retell and Book Talks Note-Taking Guide

	Retell	Book Talks
LM OW	long, overly detailed	
CF RL	short, accurate	
FS MO		Followed format -partner excited
SG CS	great sequence - wrong character names	
SW WC		Followed format, but gave ending away
CL JM	Struggled w/ sequence + setting	

Figure 6.11

The students were excited to get started with book talks and retelling. As we observed their conversations, some students disagreed over who got to do the book talk or retelling for the first book. We clarified this by suggesting the owner of the book could start the conversation, but the partner should have just as much input with the questions, comments, and connections. We overheard some strong retellings and book talks with excited responses and comments from partners. Olivia said, "I agree with you, but I also think you could recommend it because the pictures are really cool."

The most commonly observed challenge was an overly detailed retell or summary for book talks. When Landon asked his partner for questions, comments, and connections, Saige said, "That was like a twelve finger retell, not five." She was right, and Landon was not the only student who gave too many details of what happened in the story. We conferred with these partners and revisited suggestions for concise summaries. One example that worked well for Landon was, "Try to think what you would draw if you had three boxes for beginning, middle, and end. You only have three, so tell us just the three most important parts." The retelling and book talks became part of their partner reading routine quickly and with relative ease for most students, but we continued to confer and support certain partnerships during their conversations, as needed.

MONITORING AND REFINING

1. After your students are independent with book talks and retellings, release responsibility to students while you work with small groups.

2. Encourage students to talk throughout partner reading, in addition to talking at the end of the book. Encourage an option of more open-ended conversations by collaboratively creating a chart about ideas for conversations, like the one in Figure 6.12.

3. Use the 90 Seconds Partner Reading Observational Checklist in Figure 6.13 for observations. This is a modification of the original partner checklist and includes the same coding of S, N, or blank used with coaching for talking options. Use daily initially, but then shift to a weekly check-in as students settle into their partner reading routines.

4. Periodically meet with the class to have a brief reflection about partner reading time.

5. Stay on the same partnership-changing schedule as discussed in the coaching section.

Figure 6.12 Evan and Lacie sit side by side with a partner book on their laps. Lacie stops reading, references the partner reading chart beside them, and asks Evan to talk about the characters.

Peek into Our Classroom

Most students successfully used retelling or book talks after the first week of support and conferring. Students shared a book talk they rehearsed during partner reading with their table group before book shopping each week. The interest in shopping for books that had been featured significantly increased. Students were borrowing, sharing, and asking friends to hold the book for them. This generated more excitement about practicing book talks during partner reading. We modified the original 90

Seconds Partner Reading Observational Checklist to a newer version seen in Figure 6.13 to add new areas of focus (talking, retelling, and book talks) and remove areas that needed little attention at this point (one reading the whole time, equal relationships, paper/rock/scissors, etc.).

We were pleased with the success of talking after reading, but noticed there was very little talk going on during reading, and the after-reading conversations were becoming a bit formulaic. Even after prompting, we saw little to no related talk during reading with partners. We checked in with the students after two weeks to share our

90 Seconds Partner Reading Observational Checklist: Conversing Monitoring and Refining

	Choral reading	Taking turns	Silent	Both see book	2 different books	Transition	Related talk	Off-task	Coaching- Time	Coaching- Fix Up Strat	Coaching- Expression	Conversing- Book Talk	Conversing- Retell	Conversing- Informal
LM OW		1		1					S	S		S		
CF RL		1		1							S		N	
FS MO							1							
SG CS		1		1			1							S
SW WC		1									S			
CL JM		1		1									S	
TM MS		1		1								N		
SR JE								1						
ER WL			1		1									
MN AB	1			1								N		
DG CR		1		1								S		S
BB KL					1									
AK AS		1									S		S	
LB ZB		1		1										

S= Successfully Coaching or Conversing
N= Needs Support

Figure 6.13

observations with them, revisit expectations, and ask them to reflect on how it was going. Together we created an anchor chart documenting ideas for more informal conversations about books they were reading as an alternative option to the book talk or formal retell. The "Partner Reading" anchor chart in Figure 6.12 resulted from students brainstorming questions and thinking that could be shared with partners. We took their ideas that spanned two chart pages and turned them into the bookmark seen in Figure 6.14. This gave a renewed excitement and freedom to the partner talk opportunities.

DEEPENING

1. Review the talk options (book talk, retell, informal literary conversations).

2. Share observations from partner reading related to discussions about the book and students' thinking during reading.

3. Review and remind students of the multiple ways to document their thinking during independent reading (sticky notes or reading response journal entries with connections, questions, inferences, noticings, author's message, character traits, and so on). This is addressed in greater detail in Chapters 4 and 5.

4. Model reading with a partner and sharing thinking by discussing prewritten sticky notes in the book.

5. Model discussing and collaboratively creating a sticky note to document important thinking.

6. Ask students to discuss their best thinking from a previously created sticky note and document new thinking on a sticky note during partner reading.

7. Observe using the updated observational checklist in Figure 6.16.

8. Ask students to debrief and reflect on their conversations during partner reading.

Peek into Our Classroom

William and Valentina both had copies of *That Is Not a Good Idea!* (Willems 2013) with many sticky notes throughout because they were preparing for a literature discussion

Partner Talk

- What was the book about?
  *Five Finger Retell

- Did you like the book? Why?

- What was your favorite part?

- Did anything make you smile or laugh?

- Describe the characters.

- Who was your favorite character? Why?

- Did you have any connections?

- What was the author's message?

- Did you learn something new?

- Did you wonder about anything?

- Did anything confuse you?

Figure 6.14 Partner Talk bookmark

group later that week. They were excited to share their thinking. In Figure 6.15, Valentina looked on as William documented a new noticing based on their conversation. This was an example of a conversation where the students agreed and shared thinking.

We also saw some healthy disagreements, particularly when partners were reading books that required making inferences. *I Want My Hat Back* (Klassen 2011) and accompanying documentation of inferencing and character traits caused deep thinking with disagreements. We overheard the following conversation when Aubri and Farah were talking about the book.

Farah: I think a character trait for the rabbit is that he was a liar. (*She shows her sticky note to her partner.*)

Aubri: Yeah, but it doesn't mean it was okay for the bear to kill him.

Farah: The bear didn't kill him. He is just sitting on him!

Aubri: No way! He ate him. He is a liar now, too. Look (*goes back to the pages in the text where the rabbit was lying and where the bear was lying*), it's like he is talking

Figure 6.15 Valentina and William read and share their documented thinking from sticky notes. William asks Valentina to wait before continuing so he can write down a new noticing about the author's message.

too much saying what he didn't do. Like the rabbit said he didn't steal the hat, now he is saying he didn't eat the rabbit. He killed him.

Farah: (*looks horrified as she examines the pages and Aubri's inferencing sticky note that says the bear ate the rabbit*). Oh no! The bear ate the rabbit. I'm gonna write that down on a sticky note.

These were two examples of thoughtful conversations and collaborative documentation of thinking. However, a couple of partnerships appeared to be on-task, but instead were having surface-level conversations; they read their sticky notes with no discussion, which we noted on our updated observational checklist in Figure 6.16. We conferred, coached, and revisited opportunities for facilitating meaningful conversations with these partners. We also found the depth of conversations greatly depended on the type of books they were reading. Informational texts facilitated many questions and sharing of background information or connections to texts, and narrative texts provided opportunities for thinking and talking about the author's message and character traits. There was not much to talk about with decodable texts that did not have a storyline, so we discussed this with students when we debriefed after their talk experiences. After a week, we saw strong conversations for the majority of students when we completed our weekly observational checklist.

ASSESSING

Partner reading and talking is always a work in progress that requires continued revisiting, tweaking, and enhancing to make it meaningful for primary readers, but we found ways to make the assessment/observation quick and manageable. Although our richest assessment data came from the open-ended observations, notes, and conferring sessions, the observational checklist was a quick and effective means to inform our instruction. This checklist included observation for general expectations, coaching, and talking to allow for efficiency when assessing partner reading. Throughout the year, routines broke down or needed revisiting, and this checklist allowed us to document those needs without consuming large amounts of time.

We slightly modified our observational checklist to include talk during partner reading and sticky note conversations. To document if the students needed support or were successful without us, the Conversing-During column was used. However, we were also interested in the type of talk/sticky note conversations that were taking place, so we created an additional column to document what they were discussing. You can see the coding for this at the bottom of the updated chart in Figure 6.16.

Final Partner Reading 90 Seconds Observational Checklist

	Choral reading	Taking turns	Silent	Both see book	2 different books	Transition	Related talk	Off-task	Coaching- Time	Coaching- Fix Up Strat	Coaching- Expression	Conversing- Book Talk	Conversing- Retell	Conversing- Informal	Conversing- During	Sticky Conversations
LM OW																AM
CF RL		i		\						S						
FS MO		i		\												
SG CS																CT
SW WC								|								
CL JM		|		|												AM
TM MS		|		|									S			
SR JE		(		|												C
ER WL		\		|						N						
MN AB					|											Q
DG CR						(										
BB KL	|			|												L

S=Successful Independence; N=Needs Support; Blank= Not observed
Sticky Conversations: C=Connections; F=Fix-Up Strategies; I=Inferences; Q=Questions;
AM=Author's Message; CT=Character Traits; N=Noticings; L=I learned

Figure 6.16

Considerations in kindergarten and second grade

	Teacher Modifications	Student Expectations
K	· Provide additional support for conversations with sentence starters or specific comprehension considerations like character's feelings, making connections, and so on. · Provide a greater emphasis on multiple options for approximated reading (pictures, design features, retelling, and reading the words). · Support selecting books that could facilitate meaningful conversations (not repetitive, decodable texts). · Introduce modified retelling and book talks.	· Use approximated reading to participate in partner reading and discussions. · Retell and discuss stories. · Share documented thinking and strategies with partners.
2	· Encourage more complex documentation of thinking and sharing (additional supporting evidence and/or documenting thinking across multiple texts). · Quickly introduce initial talk strategies of retell and book talk. · Move quickly into introducing more-sophisticated conversations related to strategies or oral book reviews with ratings and recommendations (similar to those on Amazon or Good Reads).	· Participate in more in-depth conversations about text with interpretive responses (theme, moral, analysis, critique, and so on). · Create and share book reviews and recommendations. · Independently talk about literary elements and considerations with partner.

Calendar

	Week 1	Week 2	Week 3	Week 4	Week 5	Week 6	Week 7–Dec.	Jan.	Feb.–June
Observational checklist				X	X	X	X	X	X
Open-ended observation guide				X					
Introduce partner retelling				X					
Introduce book talks					X				
Introduce sharing sticky notes						X			
Introduce talking							X		
Needs-based small groups				X	X	X	X	X	X
Partner conferring				X	X	X	X	X	X

7 · Small-Group Experiences that Foster Collaborative Independence

Cameron stands on her tippy-toes as her fingers graze over the spines, wondering which book will be pulled for literature discussions. We purposely keep our literature discussion sets just a little out of reach but within the students' sight line to build anticipation and excitement for each book. This tactic definitely worked on Cameron. She pleads, "Can we please read The True Story of the Three Little Pigs?" *We smile and nod. She runs up and throws her arms around us. Many of her friends feel the same when we announce the choices for discussion groups. They all want to be a part of this week's fairy tale study.*

Once students choose their literature discussion book for the week, they set out on a mission, to dig deep into the text and bring their best thinking back to the group. We give the students time to read, reread, and develop their thoughts. When we pull discussion groups, Cameron shares the same enthusiasm she did on the initial book reveal day. Her book is loaded with different-colored sticky notes and she is ready to talk!

The conversation moves rapidly from student to student as all share their best thinking. The conversation heats up when Julia boldly asserts, "I don't believe him! Wolves and foxes are sneaky characters. They always lie. Don't you remember what happened to the Gingerbread Man?" Shaun politely disagrees with her, stating, "All he wanted was a cup of sugar for his granny." Cameron chimes in, "The third little pig was really rude. He told the wolf his granny could sit on a pin. I believe the wolf." Julia stands by her statement. "It's just what he wants you to think. He is telling the story and I don't think we can trust him." The conversation continues as students pull evidence from the text to support their point of view. Students notice tiny details, make connections from text to text, and infer meaning, but most importantly, they are independently engaged in a meaningful conversation about text.

Literature discussion groups are an opportunity to construct understanding as a community of readers. Students may not always agree, but they value and respect each other's thinking, preparing them for a future filled with differing opinions.

🐜 🐜 🐜

Independent small-group collaboration is a major accomplishment in the primary grades. There are many options for small groups, but we focused on student-directed literature discussion groups and performance groups. Small-group collaboration took more support, maintenance, and time to become meaningful and independent than any of our other purposeful learning experiences. We share this not to discourage you, but to support you in persevering through the initially challenging and time-consuming work. Getting five to six young children to have meaningful interactions with texts and each other without teacher support is so rewarding that we promise it is worth the work!

When primary teachers begin to foster these small-group experiences, we often hear the following questions:

- What is there to talk about when the books are at a low complexity level?
- How do you get students to listen to each other and stay on topic?
- Is it feasible for students this young to participate in discussion groups?

- How do you manage challenging behaviors or kids who don't work well together?
- Can emerging decoders really prepare, rehearse, and perform without teacher support?
- How do you grade or evaluate the performances or discussion groups?
- Will my principal just think students are playing or talking?

We used these essential questions to design, scaffold, refine, and deepen independent small-group experiences. Students were not independent in the beginning stages with discussion groups, so much of the initial scaffolding and refining took place during small-group instruction one day a week. However, once they demonstrated independence with support, they took responsibility for running and managing this opportunity once a week. These experiences also relied heavily on the purposeful learning experiences presented in the previous chapters. Without strong routines, strategy use, and independent and partner reading experiences, students will struggle to be successful with small-group independence.

Supporting Research: Why Is It Important? Does It Really Work?

There are many reasons to provide small-group instruction. Small groups allow for differentiation and interest-based interactions. We drew on small-group instruction to facilitate opportunities that eventually took place independent of the teacher. During discussion groups, we wanted children to collaboratively scaffold each other's meaning making without any particular student having a position of authority (Johnston 2004; Peterson and Eeds 1990). For this reason, we encouraged interactive conversation and did not assign roles. We provided opportunities for students to respond in various ways including analytical, intertextual, personal, transparent, and performative responses (Sipe 2007). Research demonstrates the multiple benefits of discussion groups: students engage in higher-level thinking, clarify their understanding, apply comprehension strategies, and build and share knowledge together (Kelley and Clausen-Grace 2013; Roche 2015). Discussion groups allow students of all backgrounds and reading abilities to have rich conversations following "regular opportunities to engage with books from a transactional perspective" (Martínez-Roldán and López-Robertson 1999, 279).

The second type of independent collaboration in a small group included performance. These groups participated in repeated readings and rehearsal and performed multiple types of literature (poetry, scripts, and so on). These experiences promoted fluency through repeated readings and a focus on prosody. Multiple researchers have reported a strong connection between expressive oral reading and proficient silent reading comprehension (Danne et al. 2005; National Center for Education Statistics 1995). Instructional methods that include repeated readings, such as those found when rehearsing for performances and reader's theatre, increase overall reading achievement (National Institute of Child Health and Human Development 2000; Rasinski and Hoffman 2003; Young and Rasinski 2009). We used this research to prioritize opportunities for students to work in small groups to enhance their independent reading and meaning making with peers.

Discussion Groups

Options for discussion groups are endless. Discussion groups can facilitate conversations that push students to think more deeply about what they read (Moses, Ogden, and Kelly 2015). We knew supporting meaningful discussions would be challenging. We also worried that the groups would struggle to maintain these types of conversations independently. Discussion group independence relied on multiple factors: book selection, preparation, and expectations and norms for talking in a small-group setting. Book selection is crucial to any discussion group. Although *Brown Bear, Brown Bear, What Do You See?* (Martin and Carle 1996) works well for reading repetitive and predictable text, there isn't much to talk about in a discussion group. No one will be surprised by or disagree with what happens in the story. There are no opportunities to

Title	Author	Purpose	Difficulty
Don't Let the Pigeon Drive the Bus!	Mo Willems	Humor, author's craft, character traits	Medium
Don't Let the Pigeon Stay Up Late	Mo Willems	Humor, author's craft, character traits	Medium
Pigs Make Me Sneeze	Mo Willems	Humor, author's craft, character traits, easy text for beginning readers, reader's theatre (fluency)	Low
Waiting Is Not Easy	Mo Willems	Humor, author's craft, character traits, easy text for beginning readers, reader's theatre (fluency)	Low

Figure 7.1

continues

Figure 7.1 *continued*

Title	Author	Purpose	Difficulty
Lilly's Purple Plastic Purse	Kevin Henkes	Making connections, wondering about words (vocabulary)	High (challenging vocabulary)
Chester's Way	Kevin Henkes	Making connections, wondering about words (vocabulary)	High (challenging vocabulary)
Please Mr. Panda	Steve Antony	Author's message, easy text for beginning readers	Low
You Are (Not) Small	Anna Kang	Author's message, easy text for beginning readers, author's craft, fluency/expression	Low
This Is Not My Hat	Jon Klassen	Making inferences, perspective	Low
I Want My Hat Back	Jon Klassen	Making inferences, perspective	Medium
Stand Tall Molly Lou Melon	Patty Lovell	Author's message, character traits, social/critical conversations	High
Recess Queen	Alexis O'Neil	Author's message, character traits, social/critical conversations	High
That Is Not a Good Idea!	Mo Willems	Author's craft, making inferences	Low/medium
The True Story of the Three Little Pigs	Jon Scieska	Fractured fairy tale, compare and contrast, character traits, wondering about words, perspective	High
Prince Cinder	Babette Cole	Fractured fairy tale, compare and contrast, perspective	Medium
Goldilocks and the Three Dinosaurs	Mo Willems	Fractured fairy tale, compare and contrast, perspective, wondering about words, author's craft	Medium
This Book Just Ate My Dog	Richard Byrne	Postmodern picture book, author's craft, noticings	Medium
Exclamation Mark	Amy Krouse Rosenthal	Author's message, fluency/expression/prosody, punctuation, author's craft	Medium
Swimmy	Leo Lioni	Author's message, wondering about words, problem-solution	High
Fish Is Fish	Leo Lioni	Author's message, wondering about words, problem-solution	High

Figure 7.1 *continued*

Title	Author	Purpose	Difficulty
Where the Wild Things Are	Maurice Sendak	Making inferences, reality vs. fantasy, character traits, noticings	Medium
Doctor Desoto	William Steig	Author's message, problem–solution, wondering about words, character traits	High
Click Clack Moo	Doreen Cronin	Perspective, problem–solution, making inferences	High
I Don't Want to Be a Frog	Dev Petty	Author's message, fluency/expression, author's craft, noticings	Medium
What Do You Do with a Tail Like This?	Steve Jenkins	Nonfiction text features, pulling key details, asking questions	Medium
Volcanoes	Anne Schreiber	Nonfiction text features, pulling key details, asking questions	Medium
Planets	Elizabeth Carney	Nonfiction text features, pulling key details, asking questions	Medium
Animal Hair	Sandra Markle	Nonfiction text features, pulling key details, asking questions	High

infer. Inferences create the best foundation for discussions. There are many options for text selection, but you can see the sample chart with titles, author, purpose, and difficulty level we used in our classroom in Figure 7.1.

Student preparation prior to participating in discussion group makes or breaks the experience. Students should have completed the reading and have some documented preparation (sticky notes and comprehension documentation described in Chapters 4 and 5). Students also need to know the expectations for conversations (turn taking, eye contact, making connections, adding to previous talk). These components took a great deal of time to introduce and support, but by the second half of the year, we had at least one discussion group that could run independently.

PREASSESSING

1. Use five or six text set options to create small discussion groups and let students select a book group.
2. Ask students to read the book at least once during independent reading that week.

3. Have students meet with their group to discuss the book.

4. Informally assess the following:

    a. students' preparation for book club (sticky notes, responses)

    b. types of talk (interpretive vs. literal)

    c. ways of interacting.

5. Observe students using the Discussion Group Note-Taking Guide (Figure 7.2).

Discussion Group Note-Taking Guide

	Preparation	Types of Talk	Ways of Interacting
Claudia	none	Literal: ı Interpretive:	-not talking w/ out prompting -looking off
Adan	-Question - character trait	Literal: ıı Interpretive:	talking when others asked him
Leo	- noticing - author's message	Literal: ı Interpretive: ı	- looking off - chimed in w/ short responses
Dax	- author's message	Literal: ıı Interpretive: ıı	- kept conversation going
Evelynn	- author's message -character trait - question - noticing	Literal: ııı Interpretive: ııı	- dominating talk - interrupting

Figure 7.2 Discussion Group Note-Taking Guide

We carefully selected texts we thought would be engaging, and students noted their first and second choice. We attempted to put everyone in a group they selected. We told students to read the book as one of their independent reading books at least once during the week because they were going to meet with their discussion group on Thursday. On Thursday, we said, "Everyone is going to get to be part of a discussion group. You meet with other friends who read and respond to the same book. You are going to get together and talk about the book, just like adults do. There is no assignment, just get together and discuss the book." They looked slightly baffled, but quickly got into their groups.

We thought we had selected such interesting texts that the students would have engaging conversations about them, but our assumption was incorrect. Some of the students had sticky notes in their book, but others did not. The following was a conversation overheard in one group:

Evelynn: Okay, let's get started. Dax, pay attention! I really liked the book.

(*Long silent pause. Claudia looks down at her book, and Adan and Leo look around the room. Dax plays with his book.*)

Evelynn: Come on, you guys. You have to talk about it too.

Dax: Yea, I liked it too.

Adan: (*Nods yes.*)

(*Another long pause*)

Evelynn: Leo and Claudia. You didn't say anything.

Leo: I liked it too.

Claudia: (*Nods yes.*)

This conversation was similar to what we heard in other groups. We had a lot of work to do to prepare students to have meaningful independent discussion groups.

TEACHING

1. Sit in a circle.
2. Share your observations about discussion groups with your students.
3. Create an anchor chart to address expectations for discussion interactions. See Figure 7.3 for an adaptation we created from a listen and respond strategy (Serravallo 2015).

4. Model having a whole-group discussion about a topic of interest (not necessarily related to a book).

5. Emphasize expectations for interactions.

6. Debrief and explain that whole-class literature discussions will happen daily after independent reading.

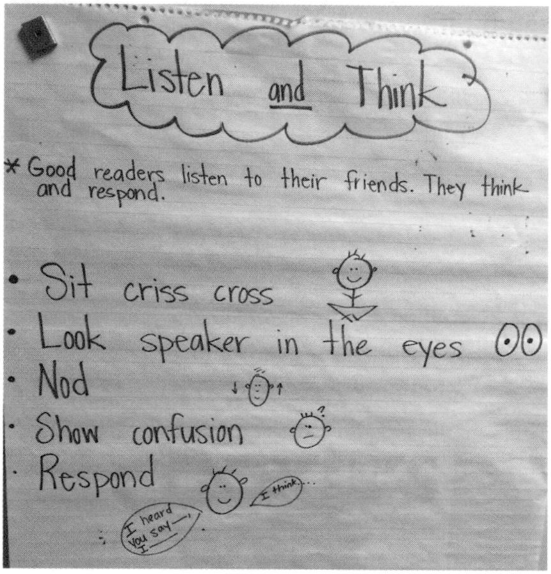

Peek into Our Classroom

We shared our observations (without names) with students. We said, "Listening and responding to our friends can be hard. We need to practice. We are going to start with some whole-group discussions first to make sure we have the hang of it before we try to do it alone in small groups again." Students generated the first two expectations, related to sitting and eye contact, for the anchor chart in Figure 7.3. We wanted to be explicit, so we added and modeled the nodding, showing confusion, and opportunities for verbal responses. We emphasized that they needed to listen so they could connect their comment to the previous speaker.

Figure 7.3 The "Listen and Think" chart was co-created with student input after we tried our first discussion groups.

To practice the interactional expectations, we chose a topic that would generate strong opinions, but not require reading preparation. We said, "Today we are going to practice the discussion group expectations with a topic everyone cares about. First, we scan the circle to make sure everyone is looking at us when we speak. If you want to add something, please place your thumb on your heart so we know you want to talk. The speaker will call on you. Everyone will look at you while you talk. Then, you will call on the next speaker with their thumb on their heart. We are going to start by saying we think kids and teachers should be in school all year long." There was a loud buzz of responses.

We redirected students to the anchor chart and reminded them to signal when they wanted to contribute. We called on Emily. She said, "That is crazy!" We asked her to tell us more and give us some support for what she said. As she started to speak, three students were still talking and many were not looking at her. We interrupted her and said, "Emily, please scan the circle for eye contact. If someone isn't ready, just say 'Excuse me' and their name." We continued with this process for about ten minutes.

During that time, we reminded students to scan the circle to make eye contact before speaking, connect to what the previous speaker said, and look at the speaker (not the teachers). It was difficult for students to follow the expectations. It was new. They were excited. We provided support and reminders for nearly every speaker on that first day. When the students debriefed after the experience, they were able to identify the challenges and reminders, which we asked them to keep in mind because they would be in reading discussion groups daily.

SCAFFOLDING

1. Have students select one book with their best thinking/sticky notes from independent reading to bring to the whole-group literature discussion.

2. Review the anchor chart about interaction expectations.

3. Facilitate a whole-group literature discussion by having a student introduce her book and share her best thinking. The student then asks for questions, comments, or connections and calls on students with their thumbs raised.

4. After three contributions, the speaker calls on a new student to share his thinking and facilitate discussion.

5. Provide continued feedback about responses and interaction expectations.

6. Continue brief (five to seven minutes) literature discussions daily.

Peek into Our Classroom

We explained, "Remember how we had a discussion group about going to school all year? Well, today we are ready to try a discussion group with the books we read. After independent reading, bring one book with a sticky note with your best thinking. Choose one you think other people will want to talk about. These are the best for getting discussion started." Students sat in a circle and placed their selected book on the ground in front of them. We quickly reviewed the anchor chart and modeled ways to respond after someone shares.

We asked Aubree to share first. She began to talk, but not everyone was looking at her. We interrupted and reminded her to scan to make eye contact. She did and quickly said, "Excuse me, Cash." Once all eyes were on her, she shared, "I did a character trait. Gerald is wimpy. He is always shaking and scared. Like on this page." Many students started talking at once. We redirected and asked Aubree to get their attention. She loved to be in charge and loudly said, "Class, class!" (They responded with "Yes, yes!") You have to raise your thumbs and look me in the eyes, then you can share. Okay, questions, comments, or connections." The students raised their thumbs, but many of them were looking at us, not Aubree. We reminded students that the designated speaker takes on the role of the teacher during literature discussions. The three students shared some literal and some deep responses.

During this first day, we focused on interaction expectations with reminders about eye contact and connecting to the previous speaker's thoughts. As the students became more comfortable with the expectations, we began to focus on the depth of sharing and responses.

MONITORING AND REFINING

1. Students select text for small-group literature discussions (the teacher selects the options for student selection).

2. Students document their thinking with sticky notes during independent and partner reading that week. Tell students to have at least one deeper-thinking sticky note (author's message, inference, character traits).

3. Introduce an anchor chart about discussion groups. See Figure 7.4.

4. Model turn taking and eye contact without hand or thumb raising.

5. Support conversations and expectations. Intervene only as needed.

6. Debrief about what went well and what could make the next literature discussion better.

Peek into Our Classroom

Whole-group literature discussions became part of our daily routine, and students ran them with little to no support from us. We thought we would eliminate them as we moved to more in-depth small-group literature discussions. However, literature discussions became a forum for book recommendations and strengthening our classroom community of readers. It also set an additional purpose for

Literature Discussions

L – Listen and look at the speaker
E – Equal participation
T – Take turns
S – Sit up and show respect
        TALK!

- This reminds me of...
- I wonder...
- I don't understand...
- I agree with_____because...
- I politely disagree with___because...
- I'd like to add to...
- So, what you're saying is...
- Can you tell me more?

Figure 7.4 This "Literature Discussions" chart reminds students about expectations and includes language frames to help students participate in meaningful conversations.

independent reading. Students were ready for an additional challenge with discussion groups. We carefully selected books that would facilitate conversations about inferences, characters, and author's message. Students made their top selections, and we formed the groups. Initially, we only did two groups a week because we were concerned about management.

We met with students in these groups on Monday to tell them they needed to document their thinking with sticky notes during their independent and partner reading by Wednesday. They had to have at least one deeper-thinking sticky note to participate in the small-group literature discussion. On Wednesday and Thursday, we met with each group and went over the "Literature Discussions" anchor chart (Figure 7.4). They were familiar with the concepts from whole-group literature discussions, but there were now additional language frames. They loved using the language frames, particularly, "I politely disagree with _____ because ___." See Figures 7.5 and 7.6 for pictures of literature circle

Figure 7.5 Jordan read *I Want My Hat Back* three different times. Her discussion group preparation included author's message, character traits, and inferences.

Figure 7.6 Valentina shares her documentation and shows the group the image as supporting evidence. The rest of the group excitedly leans over to see, point, and add to her thinking.

preparation and discussions. The biggest difference was that students were no longer raising thumbs or calling on one another. They made eye contact and took turns in a natural conversational style. We modeled this, but students often raised their hands when they got excited. They also continued to look to us after each comment, especially when the conversation stalled. And some students seemed to do most of the talking while others sat quietly.

Although we originally anticipated spending a couple of weeks guiding the groups, we ended up supporting the discussions and addressing these challenges for months. We always revisited the anchor chart prior to beginning. We also tried to intervene as little as possible. Debriefing at the end of the discussions helped students reflect on what was going well and what would make the next discussion better. As Kelly said, "Some of us talked a lot. It was good talking, but maybe it would be better if Claudia talked too." We asked the group how they might make that work, and Diego said, "Maybe just say, 'What do you think, Claudia?'" We agreed and focused on that the following week. The monitoring and refining stage of discussion groups lasted a semester for most groups. Even when we moved to complete independence in the extending stage, we returned to monitoring and refining as necessary.

EXTENDING

1. Tell students that they are going to be running their own discussion groups and that you are going to stand outside the circle, observing and only intervening if absolutely necessary.

2. Step out of the small-group discussion and complete the Discussion Group Note-Taking Guide (Figure 7.2).

3. Share your observations and debrief about what went well and what could make the next discussion group better.

4. Continue using the note-taking guide, but reduce support (don't stay with them the entire time, run other small groups, and so on).

Peek into Our Classroom

We wanted students to deepen their literature discussions and really become independent. We selected two groups of students who were reading Jon Klassen books, *I Want My Hat Back* (2011) and *This Is Not My Hat* (2012). We said, "We think you are ready to have discussion groups without our help. Today, we will stand outside your circle to listen and write down what we see. If you have a problem, you can look at the charts or work it out with your group. We are only going to talk or help if there is a big problem. You are ready to do this without us, like a real book club!" Some students looked excited and others looked nervous. We stepped back, listened, and completed our note-taking guide.

> Jonathan suggested the bear ate the rabbit, and students immediately disagree with him. Maria stated, "I think the bear is sitting on the rabbit." Juan and Jonathan both replied, "I politely disagree." Then, after Anna's prompting, the students flipped to specific pages as she provided justification by comparing text from when the rabbit was lying earlier in the story to where the bear was lying at the end. She finalized her argument by quoting text from the back cover, "Great fun, unless you are a rabbit," as evidence the rabbit was eaten. (Moses, Ogden, and Kelly 2015, 237)

This literature discussion group went smoothly. Unfortunately, they did not all work that way. We continued to observe and document students' progress with minimal input other than to debrief and provide feedback at the end. Some groups needed reminders about equal participation; others needed support with adding to conversations, preparing for discussion, or just simply getting along. In these cases, we returned to the monitoring and refining stages as necessary. When we let students choose their own group first, then collectively select a book, it seemed to mitigate many of the management and behavior challenges. To our surprise, students began to create their own groups outside of the "designated" literature discussions. They selected books with multiple classroom copies (one group brought books from home to supplement), set their own reading schedule, and asked permission to meet during partner reading. We were thrilled, and we encouraged their independent weekly meeting and discussion.

ASSESSING

Observations and the note-taking guide were vital in our assessment of students' readiness. The guide allowed us to document and provide concrete feedback on the essential components of the literature discussion groups. Literature discussion independence is challenging in the primary grades. The observational notes helped us decide when students were ready for additional responsibility and independence. We also used this assessment as a data point for their speaking and listening grades/assessment.

Alexis and Ava bounce into class, waving a stack of papers, proudly declaring, "We have a show for you! We wrote a script for I Really Like Slop!*" Other students gather around, peering over one another's shoulders to check out these two trendsetters' latest project. Justin, a Piggie and Gerald fanatic, immediately asks if he can be part of the performance group.*

Considerations in kindergarten and second grade

	Teacher Modifications	Student Expectations
K	· Provide support for accessing and decoding the text. This might include reading the text aloud in a small group, letting students listen to it on tape, or reading it together during small-group instruction. · Select specific focus for discussion group and introduce modified colored sticky notes to document their thinking (character's feelings, inference) by color without writing. · Shorten length of discussion group.	· Use oral or sketched responses to document thinking and share during literature discussions. · Take turns talking. · Make connections to the speaker.
2	· Provide less time in the teaching, scaffolding, and monitoring and refining stages. · Encourage students to generate discussion questions in addition to reading responses for preparation. · Introduce opportunities for students to conduct literature discussions across texts (similar topics, themes, genres, authors, etc.). · Introduce opportunities to conduct longer discussion groups with chapter books (may take 2–4 weeks to complete the reading, but group meets weekly to discuss). · Provide extended time for discussion groups. · Can run three or four groups per week.	· Read more complex text that extends reading for more than a week. · Use reading responses from extended texts with deeper comprehension strategies to discuss and analyze change over time in chapter books. · Generate inferential, critical, and analytic questions to help deepen literature discussions. · Collaborate with peers to establish expectations and successful discussion groups.

Calendar

	Week 1	Week 2	Week 3	Week 4	Week 5	Week 6	Week 7–Dec.	Jan.	Feb.–June
Introduce literature discussion expectations				X					
Introduce whole-group literature discussions				X					
Introduce small-group literature discussions with teacher support						X			
Conduct independent small-group literature discussions								X	X
Use note-taking guide to assess discussion groups				X	X	X	X	X	X

Many students follow suit, pleading to be part of what is sure to be a performance hit.

We settle the children in for partner reading and invite Ava and Alexis to come up and officially share the script with the class. Ava describes their thought process and asks who wanted to be a part of their performance. Hands fly up and eager eyes hone in on the girls. They only need one additional performer, so the choice is challenging. Ava thoughtfully chooses Evan to play the role of the flies, and, of course, the two cowriters will play the leading roles of Piggie and Gerald. Ava pauses for a moment and states, "We could use a director to help keep us on track." Alexis quickly picks William, but reassures the rest of her classmates they will be writing more scripts, so there will be other opportunities.

The four children scurry to the back of the classroom to practice. William keeps the group organized and on track, provides performance feedback about prosody and intonation, and shares ideas for hand motions and body movements. We check in and suggest facing the audience and lowering their scripts. It is a quick visit because they really don't need our assistance. They are joyfully and independently guiding their own learning.

Other partners pull out their Piggie and Gerald books and begin transcribing their own scripts. We hear many high-pitched Piggie squeals of excitement and low-tone Gerald moans of anxiety. The magic has begun and a new reading trend has organically grown. They are reading with great intent as they prepare to wow their classmates with future performances.

Performance groups were an instant success. They fostered creativity while supporting students' ability to read with great accuracy, prosody, and intonation. We quickly learned that the art of putting on a good show creates a great sense of purpose for young learners.

Performance Groups

There are so many options for performance groups, ranging from presenting research to performing poetry or reader's theatre scripts. Opportunities for performance create a sense of purpose and authenticity when students work on repeated readings and prosody. Research has documented the many benefits to repeated readings and reader's theatre for fluency and comprehension (National Institute of Child Health and Human Development 2000; Rasinski and Hoffman 2003; Young and

Rasinski 2009). Not to mention, the kids *loved* their performance groups! These groups developed independence much quicker and with greater ease than discussion groups.

A combination of opportunities to perform kept our students engaged and excited. Small groups reduced the stress and anxiety some students experience when speaking or performing in front of their peers. One small-group performance option included rehearsing and giving feedback on individual performances, such as poetry performances. Another option included collaborative rehearsal with students having parts or roles in a script that would eventually be performed for the class or another small group.

PREASSESSING

1. Tell students to practice reading aloud or performing a poem (one they have in the folder or one they created) during independent and/or partner reading because they will perform with their small group this week.

2. Ask students to read the poem aloud to their small group.

3. Observe using the Poetry Performance Rubric in Figure 7.7.

Peek into Our Classroom

We were in the middle of a reading and writing poetry unit, so a poetry performance opportunity was a perfect fit. We told students, "Poetry is meant to be read aloud and

Student name:			
	Got It!	**Almost There**	**Still Working**
Volume	Loud enough for everyone in the group to hear	Loud enough for most members to hear	Many members unable to hear
Speaks Clearly	Speaks clearly and pronounces the words correctly	Speaks clearly and pronounces the words correctly some of the time	Is difficult to understand and has trouble pronouncing words
Expression	Uses tone to read with feeling	Changes in tone used periodically	Reads in a monotone voice
Speed	Not too fast, not too slow	Sometimes too fast or too slow	Too fast or too slow for the entire poem
Eye Contact	Periodically looks at the audience	Looks at the audience only before and/or after performance	Does not look at the audience

Figure 7.7 Poetry Performance Rubric

performed. This week you are going to get your first chance to do that. During independent and partner reading, practice reading one poem with expression to eventually perform for a small group." We explained the poem could be one they wrote for writer's workshop, a class poem that is in their reading folder, or a poem from a poetry book.

At the end of the week, students performed their poem to their table groups. Some students were very animated and excited, but the majority of students just looked at their poem and read it aloud in a monotone voice. We quickly highlighted the poetry performance rubric. Eye contact, expression, and volume needed the most attention.

TEACHING

1. Ask students to identify what makes a good poetry performance.

2. Share your observations about the performances with your students.

3. Create an anchor chart to address poetry performance tips. Figure 7.8 shows an example.

4. Model or show a video of a poetry performance.

5. Have students give feedback related to the poetry performance tips.

6. Discuss what makes a good performance audience.

7. Create an anchor chart to address performance audience tips. Figure 7.9 shows an example.

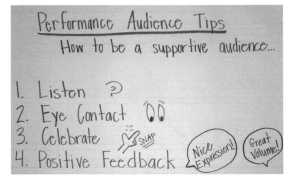

Figure 7.8 The students helped created the "Poetry Performances" chart that focused on volume, clarity, expression, speed, and eye contact.

Figure 7.9 The students shared their thinking about how to be a good performance audience member. We used this input to create the "Performance Audience Tips" chart.

Peek into Our Classroom

After the initial, unsupported poetry performance, we asked students what made a good poetry performance. Shaun said, "Not reading like a robot." We agreed, and asked, "What *should* the performer do?" Shaun said, "Read with a fun voice." We emphasized that students should read with expression. Other ideas the students generated included appropriate volume and speed. Barrett said, "Like a just-right book, but with reading—not too loud, not too soft, not too fast, not too slow!" We shared our observations, and together we created the anchor chart in Figure 7.8 to document poetry performance tips.

Students worked in poetry performance groups for weeks in preparation for our coffeehouse performances, a culminating event of the poetry unit where we stage the room like four coffeehouses and the students perform a selected piece in small groups. We asked students to consider the poetry performance tips as they viewed a video of student poetry performance (Asha Christensen at TEDxKids@SMU 2012 is a great one; see https://www.youtube.com/watch?v=rtnEnEqjk0E). They unanimously agreed that Asha used all the tips we created.

Next, students generated ideas about what a good audience group member should do during a performance. They immediately identified eye contact, being quiet, and listening. We added snapping fingers in celebration of the performance and providing some type of verbal feedback. We asked students to turn and talk about positive feedback with supporting evidence from the performance related to our anchor chart. Jordan said, "She did a really good job with expression and speed. Her voice changed a lot and she slowed down and sped up just right."

SCAFFOLDING

1. Tell students to practice performing a poem during independent and/or partner reading at least once a day to prepare for a performance later in the week.

2. Review the anchor chart about poetry performance tips.

3. Confer with students throughout the week to provide feedback.

4. Remind students about audience expectations.

5. Have students perform in table groups of four or five with audience feedback.

6. Debrief about what went well and what they can do to make their performances better.

Peek into Our Classroom

Students were excited when we told them they would be working on their poetry performances. We quickly reviewed the poetry performance tips and asked students to select one poem from their folder or one they created to be the focus of their rehearsal and performance that week. We said, "Remember Asha's performance? Use some of the strategies that you liked in her performance. Practice like you are performing because you will get to perform at the end of the week." About half the class chose a published poem, and the other half chose poems they had written.

Barrett, who naturally has a flare for the dramatic, loudly projected his voice with a great deal of intonation and accompanying arm movements. He wanted to rehearse during the entire independent reading time. However, Isha and Ava asked him to be quiet multiple times. We decided to carve out a short time during independent reading for rehearsal so others weren't distracted. We gave students the first three to five minutes of independent reading to rehearse, but returned to normal independent reading expectations for the remainder of the session. We gave students the same amount of time at the beginning of partner reading and asked them to give their partners feedback.

Barrett said to Aiden, "You gotta make it exciting, like me!" We chimed in to reassure Aiden that his performance could use more expression and volume, but that every performer has their own style. Students were excited and prepared for their performances. Even our shyest students performed at a volume that the other children could hear. Students provided positive feedback to each other and loved snapping their fingers at the completion of each poem. We debriefed and asked students what went well and what they could do to make it better the following week. Everyone agreed that the expression and volume was better. Alexis added, "Some people could probably try to look up more." We continued with this poetry focus through the whole unit. It became a rotation during small-group time that students ran independently. While we were working in instructional small groups, another small group would be practicing and/or giving feedback for a poetry performance. We eventually published a class book with one piece of performed poetry from every student.

MONITORING AND REFINING

1. Create or find appropriate reader's theatre scripts (see www.thebestclass.org /rtscripts.html for free scripts).

2. Introduce the scripts and discuss preparation for a group performance.

3. Give students small-group rehearsal time. (This can take the place of partner reading.)

4. Provide feedback and support as needed.

5. Have students perform for the class or other small group.

6. Debrief about what went well and what could make the next performance better.

Peek into Our Classroom

By the end of the poetry unit, students were losing interest in the poetry performances. They were also ready for a greater challenge—working with peers for a small-group performance. We knew it would be challenging to shift from individual performances in a small-group setting to group performances. We wanted to keep it simple, so we created scripts for the students based on some of their favorite, multicharacter books by Mo Willems. We did this for two reasons. We knew students had been exposed to the texts and storylines, and they could use the book and pictures to help support their dialogue and rehearsal if the words were challenging.

Students worked with friends to rehearse a play they would perform for the class. We showed them how to navigate a script. The first time, we highlighted the parts in different colors so they could associate themselves with a character (and a color for easy identification). Twice a week students worked with their performance groups during partner reading while we were instructing small groups. We periodically conferred with students, gave feedback, and encouraged them to give each other feedback. We overheard Evelynn say, "That's not what Gerald would sound like. It has to be kinda wimpy, like this" (a shaky, high-pitched voice). Students needed little to no support by this point because much of the work was rehearsal and repeated readings that came with the support of peers, a familiar script, and accompanying picture book.

As students' rehearsals became fluent, we asked them to create props to help enhance their performance. Figure 7.10 shows Aubree, Owen, and Aidan doing a final rehearsal with props. Aubree and Owen were reluctant readers who often

Figure 7.10 Aubree encouraged Owen and Aiden to speak louder and use more expression during their reader's theatre rehearsal.

read choppily, but the repeated readings helped them develop stronger fluency and confidence in reading aloud. The small-group audience loved their performance and cheered loudly upon its completion. Initially, we had students perform for another small group of students, but we also had some small groups perform for the whole class.

EXTENDING

1. Tell students they are going to be making their own scripts for performances.

2. Model whole-class interactive script writing (students can create a script for a familiar story, or make up their own).

3. Allow students to self-select into small groups for script writing.

4. Support script creation during small-group time.

5. Provide time for rehearsal during partner reading with support and feedback as necessary.

6. Have students perform for the class or other small group.

Peek into Our Classroom

Students had become completely independent with running their own reader's theatre groups, if we provided scripts. We wanted them to think more deeply about the relationship between stories, texts, scripts, and performances (we also wanted them to continue enjoying themselves while they further developed their fluency and confidence). By this time, they understood the basic components of scripts. When we modeled writing a script for a familiar story, the Three Little Pigs, the students easily participated in the interactive writing.

Coordinating and being independent with script writing was another story. Some groups struggled to decide on a storyline or which book they wanted to turn into a script. They also needed additional support designating responsibilities. We said to Christian and Christopher, "Talk to us about your script. We don't see the different actors." We were looking at their copy of an early version script for *Duck! Rabbit!* (Rosenthal and Lichtenheld 2009). Christian explained, "We don't want to each have to write out the whole thing, so we are just writing our own parts. There are only two people in this story." We understood their need for efficiency, but asked, "So, how will you know when to talk and when the other person will talk?" It was clear from their faces that they hadn't thought about that. Christopher looked frustrated, but Christian chimed in, "What if I just draw a line when I stop talking? He will do his part, and when he is done, I will know I start after the line." We agreed, but suggested they would need to start putting it in one document for future scripts. We told the class that they could write one copy of the script, and we would make copies for them, or they could write or type it on a device.

Students worked diligently to write and rehearse their scripts. It became an option during partner reading and writer's workshop. Some students worked through the process multiple times, and other groups tried it once and decided they preferred partner reading and responses.

Our biggest success with the script creation and performance came from a small group that created the script for our end-of-year book awards ceremony. Their script was written with teacher assistance on a device and was performed by the whole class. It included host dialogue (the two lead writers), a musical performance, and award presentations (different students were selected to read about the category and announce the winner). Figure 7.11 shows the hosts at the awards ceremony. Figure 7.12 shows students celebrating after the winner was announced for best nonfiction, *Looking Closely: Across the Desert* (Serafini 2008). As you can see, these opportunities generated excitement and engagement with writing, reading, and performing. Most of all, students were proud because they worked through the process with collaborative independence, instead of teacher-directed options. Audience, purpose, and student voice created buy-in for digging deeper into texts, scripts, and performances with peers.

Figure 7.11 The two lead script writers and hosts, Ava and Alexis, read off the script to get the book awards ceremony started.

Figure 7.12 Jordan and Aiden are the first to jump and scream with joy when they hear that the book they voted for won the best nonfiction category.

ASSESSING

Observations and the rubric were helpful for providing feedback with poetry performances. This assessment helped support the transition into self-directed reader's theatre options. We did not use a rubric for reader's theatre performances, but many teachers need or want to have assessment data to document progress when students are spending reading time working on performances. Readwritethink.org has samples, like the one found at www.readwritethink.org/classroom-resources/printouts/readers -theatre-rubric-30698.html. Another resource we like is iRubric, with an adjustable rubric at www.rcampus.com/rubricshowc.cfm?code=K8A245&sp=true. An additional option would be an oral reading fluency scale, like the one from U.S. Department of Education, National Center for Education Statistics in *Listening to Children Read Aloud* (1995). More information on this can be found at http://nces.ed.gov/pubs95 /web/95762.asp.

Considerations in kindergarten and second grade

	Teacher Modifications	Student Expectations
K	· Provide rhyming/familiar poems or short songs that the students can perform. · Select simple texts and designate part (like one page in *Good Night Moon* [Brown and Hurd 1947] or other familiar text). · Allow additional rehearsal time. · Use illustrations to support script reading. · Encourage students to create scripts using improvisation, sketches, and performance with peers.	· Conduct repeated readings of familiar poems or short songs. · Rehearse and participate in simple reader's theatre performance. · Use comprehension and background knowledge to improvise performance when reading is too challenging.
2	· Provide more complex poetry and scripts. · Encourage students to take on multiple roles and consider using additional technology (recorded performances vs. live). · Introduce more rigorous considerations and rubrics for performance. · Ask students to provide constructive feedback on performances that includes one compliment and one area of constructive feedback related to fluency, prosody, and overall performance. · Provide early opportunities for script writing and extensions.	· Read, create, and perform more complex poetry and scripts. · Take ownership of script writing and adjustment of prewritten scripts. · Utilize technology to record performances and/ or rehearsals. · Provide constructive feedback related to fluency, prosody, and performance. · Collaborate with peers to establish expectations and successful performance groups.

Calendar

	Week 1	Week 2	Week 3	Week 4	Week 5	Week 6	Week 7–Dec.	Jan.	Feb.–June
Introduce poetry performances						X			
Use rubric to assess poetry performances						X	X	X	X
Introduce reader's theatre							X		
Introduce crafting original scripts for reader's theatre								X	X
Book awards show									X May–June

Difficulty-Level Checklist

Name	Independent	Instructional	Frustration	Frustration & High Interest

Independent Reading Observational Checklist

Name	Reading aloud	Reading silently	Tracking text	Pointing to pictures	Related talking	Looking at pictures/ cover	Getting up	Staring at one page	Playing with book	Playing with other children	Unrelated talking	Seeking adult assistance

Independent Checklist

Name	Reading aloud	Reading silently	Tracking text	Pointing to pictures	Related talking	Looking at pictures/cover	Getting up	Staring at one page	Playing with book	Playing with other children	Unrelated talking	Seeking adult assistance	Making a connection	Asking a question	Making an inference	Author's intention	Using a fix-up strategy

Small-Group Strategy Note-Taking Guide

Strategy Group Goal: **Strategy:** **Date:**	_____ without prompting.	_____ _____ with prompting and support.	Alternative strategies tried _____ _____
Name			

Comprehension Strategy Note-Taking Guide

Name	Comprehension Strategy Use										
	Visualizing	Sequencing	Five finger retell	Connections (TS, TT, TW)	"I Learned" (key ideas & details)	"I wonder"	Character traits	Noticings	Compare & contrast	Inference	Author's message

I = Inaccurate Use, *S* = Surface-Level Use, *M* = Meaningful Use

Strategy Reflection Log

		Strategy Documentation	Sticky Note (Evidence)
Summarizing	☐ Sequencing ☐ Five finger retell ☐ "I learned" (key ideas and details)		
Making Connections	☐ Text-to-self ☐ Text-to-text ☐ Text-to-world		
Inferring	☐ Inference ☐ Character traits ☐ Visualize		
Analyzing	☐ Author's message ☐ Author's craft ☐ Compare and contrast		

Reading Response Note-Taking Guide

Name	During Reading		After Reading	
	Strengths	*Needs*	*Strengths*	*Needs*

Inquiry Response and Interaction Note-Taking Guide

Names	Documented Responses/Thinking	Discussion After Reading

Research Recording Sheet

Stick to the "Big Ideas"

_____

Expert Topic

Big Idea #1	Big Idea #2
Big Idea #3	WOW Facts

Inquiry Response and Interaction Note-Taking Guide

Names	Documented Responses/Thinking	Discussion During Reading	Discussion After Reading

Partner Reading Open-Ended Note-Taking Guide

Names	What are they doing?	Who is reading?	How are they positioned?	How do they take turns?	Whose book are they reading?	What do they do when they get stuck on a word?

Partner Reading 90 Seconds Observational Checklist

Names	Choral reading	Taking turns	One reading	Silent	Both see book	Two different books	Equal relationships	One dominating	Transition	Rock, Paper, Scissors	Related talk	Unrelated talk	One off-task	Both off-task	Coaching: time	Coaching: fix-up strategies

Final Partner Reading: Coaching 90 Seconds Observational Checklist

Names	Choral reading	Taking turns	One reading	Silent	Both see book	Two different books	Equal relationships	One dominating	Transition	Rock, Paper, Scissors	Related talk	Unrelated talk	One off-task	Both off-task	Coaching: time	Coaching: fix-up strategies	Coaching: expression

S = successfully coaching; *N* = needs support.

Partner Reading: Talk Note-Taking Guide

Names	What are they talking about during reading?	Discussion after reading

Partner Reading: Retell and Book Talks Note-Taking Guide

Names	Retell	Book Talks

90 Seconds Partner Reading Observational Checklist: Talking, Monitoring, and Refining

Names	Choral reading	Taking turns	Silent	Both see book	Two different books	Transition	Related talk	Off-task	Coaching: time	Coaching: fix-up strategies	Coaching: expression	Talking: book talk	Talking: retell	Talking: informal

S= successfully coaching or talking, *N* = needs support.

Final Partner Reading 90 Seconds Observational Checklist

Names	Choral reading	Taking turns	Silent	Both see book	Two different books	Transition	Related talk	Off-task	Coaching: time	Coaching: fix-up strategies	Coaching: expression	Talking: book talk	Talking: retell	Talking: informal	Talking: during	Sticky conversations

S = successful independence; *N* = needs support; Blank = not observed. Sticky conversations: *C* = connections; *F* = fix-up strategies; *I* = inferences; *Q* = questions; *AM* = author's message; *CT* = character traits; *N* = noticings; *L* = "I learned."

Discussion Group Note-Taking Guide

Name	Preparation	Types of Talk	Ways of Interacting
		Literal: Interpretive:	
		Literal: Interpretive:	
		Literal: Interpretive:	
		Literal: Interpretive:	
		Literal: Interpretive:	

References

Allington, Richard. 2009. "If They Don't Read Much . . . 30 Years Later." In *Reading More, Reading Better,* edited by Elfrieda H. Hiebert, 30–54. New York: Guilford.

Allington, Richard L., and Patricia M. Cunningham. 2002. *Schools That Work: Where All Children Read and Write,* 2nd ed. Boston: Allyn and Bacon.

Bauso, Jean Arrington. 1988. "Incorporating Reading Logs into a Literature Course." *Teaching English in the Two-Year College* 15 (4): 255–61.

Bergeron, Bette S., and Melody Bradbury-Wolff. 2010. "'If It's Not Fixed, the Staples Are Out!' Documenting Young Children's Perceptions of Strategic Reading Processes." *Reading Horizons* 50 (1): 1–22.

Biffle, Chris. 2013. *Whole Brain Teaching for Challenging Kids (and the Rest of Your Classroom).* Yucaipa, CA. Whole Brain Teaching LLC.

Blatt, Gloria T., and Lois Matz Rosen. 1984. "The Writing Response to Literature." *Journal of Reading* 28 (1): 8–12.

Boushey, Gail, and Joan Moser. 2014. *The Daily 5: Fostering Literacy Independence in the Elementary Grades.* Portland, ME: Stenhouse.

Brown, Sally A. 2006. "Investigating Classroom Discourse Surrounding Partner Reading." *Early Childhood Education Journal* 34 (1): 29–36.

Buettner, Edwin G. 2002. "Sentence by Sentence Self-Monitoring." *The Reading Teacher* 56 (1): 34–44.

Buhrow, Brad, and Anne Upczak-Garcia. 2006. *Ladybugs, Tornadoes, and Swirling Galaxies: English Language Learners Discover Their World Through Inquiry.* Portland, ME: Stenhouse.

Calkins, Lucy. 2000. *The Art of Teaching Reading.* Needham Heights, MA: Allyn & Bacon.

———. 2010. *A Guide to the Reading Workshop.* Portsmouth, NH: Heinemann.

Chall, Jeanne S. 1983. *Stage of Reading Development.* New York: McGraw-Hill.

Clay, Marie. 1991. *Becoming Literate: The Construction of Inner Control.* Portsmouth, NH: Heinemann.

Cleaveland, Lisa. 2016. *More About the Authors.* Portsmouth, NH: Heinemann.

Collins, Kathy. 2004. *Growing Readers: Units of Study in the Primary Classroom.* Portland, ME: Stenhouse.

Collins, Kathy, and Matt Glover. 2015. *I Am Reading: Nurturing Young Children's Meaning Making and Joyful Engagement with Any Book.* Portsmouth, NH: Heinemann.

Danne, Mary C., Jay R. Campbell, Wendy S. Grigg, Madeline J. Goodman, and Andreas Oranje. 2005. "Fourth-Grade Students Reading Aloud: NAEP 2002 Special Study of Oral Reading. The Nation's Report Card. NCES 2006-469." *National Center for Education Statistics.*

Dewey, John. 1997. *Experience and Education.* New York: Free Press.

Duke, Nell. 2014. *Inside Information: Developing Powerful Readers and Writers of Informational Text Through Project-Based Instruction.* New York: Scholastic.

Duke, Nell, and Meghan Block. 2012. "Improving Reading in the Primary Grades." *The Future of Children* 22 (2): 55–72.

Flitterman-King, Sharon. 1988. "The Role of the Response Journal in Active Reading." *Quarterly of the National Writing Project and the Center for the Study of Writing* 10 (3): 4–11.

Fountas, Irene C., and Gay Su Pinnell. 2011. *The Continuum of Literacy Learning PreK–8: A Guide to Teaching,* 2nd ed. Portsmouth, NH: Heinemann.

Gandini, Lella. 2012. "Connecting Through Caring and Learning Spaces." In *The Hundred Languages,* edited by Carolyn Edwards, Lella Gandini, and George Forman, 317–41. Santa Barbara, CA: Praeger.

Griffin, Mary Lee. 2002. "Why Don't You Use Your Finger? Paired Reading in First Grade." *The Reading Teacher* 55 (8): 766–74.

Guccione [Moses], Lindsey. 2010. "An Ethnographic Approach to Examine the Community of Practice, Literacy Practices, and Construction of Meaning Among First-Grade Linguistically Diverse Learners." Doctoral dissertation. Available from Dissertations and Theses database at University of Northern Colorado (Publication No. AAT 3415987).

Halladay, Juliet L. 2008. "Reconsidering Frustration-Level Texts: Second Graders' Experiences with Difficult Texts." Paper presented at the annual meeting of the National Reading Conference, December, Orlando, FL.

———. 2012. "Revisiting Key Assumptions of the Reading Level Framework." *The Reading Teacher* 66 (1): 53–62.

Hancock, Marjorie R. 1993. "Literature Response Journals: Insights Beyond the Printed Page." *Language Arts* 69 (1): 36–42.

Harvey, Stephanie, and Harvey Daniels. 2009. *Comprehension & Collaboration: Inquiry Circles in Action.* Portsmouth, NH: Heinemann.

Heard, Georgia, and Jennifer McDonough. 2009. *A Place for Wonder: Reading and Writing Nonfiction in the Primary Grades.* Portland, MA: Stenhouse.

Hiebert, Elfrieda H., and Charles W. Fisher. 2012. "Fluency from the First: What Works with First Graders." In *Fluency Instruction: Research-Based Best Practices,* edited by Timothy Rasinski, Camille L. Z. Blachowicz, and Kristin Lems, 279–92. New York: Guilford Press.

Johnston, Peter H. 2004. *Choice Words: How Our Language Affects Children's Learning.* Portland, MA: Stenhouse.

Johnston, Peter, and Paula Costello. 2005. "Principles for Literacy Assessment." *Reading Research Quarterly* 40 (2): 256–67.

Keene, Ellin Oliver. 2008. *To Understand: New Horizons in Reading Comprehension.* Portsmouth, NH: Heinemann.

Keene, Ellin Oliver, and Susan Zimmerman. 1997. *Mosaic of Thought.* Portsmouth, NH: Heinemann.

Kelley, Michelle J., and Nicki Clausen-Grace. 2009. "Facilitating Engagement by Differentiating Independent Reading." *The Reading Teacher* 63 (4): 313–18. http://doi.org/10.1598/RT.63.4.6.

———. 2013. *Comprehension Shouldn't Be Silent: From Strategy Instruction to Student Independence,* 2nd ed. Newark, DE: International Reading Association.

Krashen, Stephen D. 1987. *Principles and Practice in Second Language Acquisition.* Englewood Cliffs, NJ: Prentice-Hall.

Martínez-Roldán, Carmen M., and Julia M. López-Robertson. 1999. "Initiating Literature Circles in a First-Grade Bilingual Classroom." *The Reading Teacher* 53 (4): 270–81.

McNaughton, Stuart. 1981. "The Influence of Immediate Teacher Correction on Self-Corrections and Proficient Oral Reading." *Journal of Reading Behavior* 13 (4): 367–71.

Meisinger, Elizabeth B., Paula J. Schwanenflugel, Barbara A. Bradley, and Steven A. Stahl. 2004. "Interaction Quality During Partner Reading." *Journal of Literacy Research* 36 (2): 111–40.

Moses, Lindsey. 2011. "Integrating Literacy and Inquiry for English Learners." *The Reading Teacher* 64 (8): 567–77.

———. 2015. *Supporting English Learners in the Reading Workshop.* Portsmouth, NH: Heinemann.

Moses, Lindsey, Meridith Ogden, and Laura Beth Kelly. 2015. "Facilitating Meaningful Discussion Groups in the Primary Grades." *The Reading Teacher* 69 (2): 233–37.

Murphy, P. Karen, Ian A. G. Wilkinson, Anna O. Soter, Maeghan N. Hennessey, and John F. Alexander. 2009. "Examining the Effects of Classroom Discussion on Students' Comprehension of Text: A Meta-Analysis." *Journal of Educational Psychology* 101 (3): 740.

National Association for the Education of Young Children and the International Reading Association. 1998. "Learning to Read and Write: Developmentally Appropriate Practices for Young Children." *Young Children* 53 (4): 30–46.

National Center for Education Statistics.1995. *Listening to Children Read Aloud, 15.* Washington, DC: U.S. Department of Education.

National Governors Association Center for Best Practices and Council of Chief State School Officers. 2010a. *Application of Common Core State Standards for English Language Learners.* Washington, DC: Author. www.corestandards.org/assets/application-for-english-learners.pdf.

———. 2010b. *Common Core State Standards for English Language Arts & Literacy in History/ Social Studies, Science, and Technical Subjects.* Washington, DC: Author.

National Institute of Child Health and Human Development. 2000. *Report of the National Reading Panel. Teaching Children to Read: An Evidence-Based Assessment of the Scientific Research Literature on Reading and its Implications for Reading Instruction* (NIH Publication No. 00-4769). Washington, DC: U.S. Government Printing Office.

Nystrand, Martin. 2006. "Research on the Role of Classroom Discourse as it Affects Reading Comprehension." *Research in the Teaching of English* 40 (4): 392–412.

Opitz, Michael F., and Lindsey Moses Guccione. 2009. *Comprehension and English Language Learners: 25 Oral Reading Strategies That Cross Proficiency Levels*. Portsmouth, NH: Heinemann.

Pearson, P. David, Janice A. Dole, Gerald G. Duffy, and Laura R. Roehler. 1992. "Developing Expertise in Reading Comprehension: What Should Be Taught and How Should It Be Taught?" In *What Research Has to Say to the Teacher of Reading,* 2nd ed., edited by Allen E. Farstup and Jay S. Samuels. Newark, DE: International Reading Association.

Peterson, Ralph, and Maryann Eeds. 1990. *Grand Conversations: Literature Groups in Action*. New York: Scholastic.

Pratt, Sharon M., and Melena Urbanowski. 2016. "Teaching Early Readers to Self-Monitor and Self-Correct." *The Reading Teacher* 69 (5): 559–67.

Rasinski, Timothy, and James V. Hoffman. 2003. "Theory and Research into Practice: Oral Reading in the School Literacy Curriculum." *Reading Research Quarterly* 38 (4): 510–22.

Reis, Sally M., Rebecca D. Eckert, D. Betsy McCoach, Joan K. Jacobs, and Michael Coyne. 2008. "Using Enrichment Reading Practices to Increase Reading Fluency, Comprehension, and Attitudes." *The Journal of Educational Research 101* (5): 299–314.

Reutzel, D. Ray, Parker C. Fawson, and John A. Smith. 2008. "Reconsidering Silent Sustained Reading: An Exploratory Study of Scaffolded Silent Reading." *The Journal of Educational Research* 102 (1): 37–50.

Roche, Mary. 2015. *Developing Young Children's Critical Thinking Through Picturebooks: A Guide for Primary and Early Years Students and Teachers*. New York: Routledge.

Rogoff, Barbara. 1990. *Apprenticeships in Thinking: Cognitive Development in Social Context*. New York: Oxford University Press.

Rosenblatt, Louise. 1978. *The Reader, the Text, the Poem*. Carbondale, IL: Southern Illinois Press.

Rupert, Pamela R., and Martha A. Brueggeman. 1986. "Reading Journals: Making the Language Connection in College." *Journal of Reading* 30 (1): 26–33.

Sanden, Sherry. 2012. "Independent Reading: Perspectives and Practices of Highly Effective Teachers." *The Reading Teacher* 66 (3): 222–231. http://doi.org/10.1002/TRTR.01120.

———. 2014. "Out of the Shadow of SSR: Real Teachers' Classroom Independent Reading Practices." *Language Arts* 91 (3): 161–75.

Serafini, Frank. 2001. *The Reading Workshop: Creating Space for Readers*. Portsmouth, NH. Heinemann.

Serafini, Frank, and Lindsey Moses. 2015. "Considering Design Features." *The Reading Teacher* 69 (3): 307–309.

Serravallo, Jennifer. 2010. *Teaching Reading in Small Groups: Differentiated Instruction for Building Strategic, Independent Readers*. Portsmouth, NH: Heinemann.

———. 2015. *The Reading Strategies Book*. Portsmouth, NH: Heinemann.

Sipe, Lawrence. 2007. *Storytime: Young Children's Literary Understandings in the Classroom*. New York: Teachers College Press.

Taberski, Sharon. 2000. *On Solid Ground: Strategies for Teaching Reading K–3*. Portsmouth, NH: Heinemann.

Taylor, Barbara M., Barbara J. Frye, and Geoffrey M. Maruyama. 1990. "Time Spent Reading and Reading Growth." *American Education Research Journal* 27 (2): 351–62.

Topping, Keith. 1989. "Peer Tutoring and Paired Reading: Combining Two Powerful Techniques." *The Reading Teacher* 42 (7): 488–94.

Trudel, Heidi. 2007. "Making Data-Driven Decisions: Silent Reading." *The Reading Teacher* 61 (4): 308–315. http://doi.org/10.1598/RT.61.4.3.

Vygotsky, Lev. 1978. *Mind in Society*. Cambridge, MA: Harvard University Press.

———. 1987. "Thinking and Speech." In *The Collected Works of S. L. Vygotsky, Volume 1: Problems of General Psychology*, edited by R. W. Riber and A. S. Carton. New York: Plenum.

Wells, Gordon. 1999. *Dialogic Inquiry: Towards a Sociocultural Practice and Theory of Education*. Cambridge, UK: Cambridge University Press.

Wright, Gary, Ross Sherman, and Timothy B. Jones. 2004. "Are Silent Reading Behaviors of First Graders Really Silent?" *The Reading Teacher* 57 (6): 546–53.

Wutz, Jessica Ann, and Linda Wedwick. 2005. "BOOKMATCH: Scaffolding Book Selection for Independent Reading." *The Reading Teacher* 59 (1): 16–32.

Yoon, Jun-Chae. 2002. "Three Decades of Sustained Silent Reading: A Meta-Analytic Review of the Effects of SSR on Attitude Toward Reading." *Reading Improvement* 39 (4): 186–95.

Young, Chase, and Timothy Rasinski. 2009. "Implementing Readers Theatre as an Approach to Classroom Fluency Instruction." *The Reading Teacher* 63 (1): 4–13.

Children's Literature

Antony, Steve. 2014. *Please, Mr. Panda*. New York: Scholastic.

Brown, Margaret Wise, and Clement Hurd. 1947. *Goodnight Moon*. New York: Harper.

Byrne, Richard. 2014. *This Book Just Ate My Dog!* New York: Henry Holt and Company.

Carl, Eric. 1996. *The Grouchy Ladybug*. New York: Harper Collins.

———. 1979. *The Very Hungry Caterpillar*. New York: Collins Publishers

Carney, Elizabeth. 2012. *Planets*. Washington, D.C.: National Geographic Society.

Cole, Babette. 1997. *Prince Cinders*. New York: Puffin Books.

Cronin, Doreen. 2000. *Click, Clack, Moo: Cows That Type*. New York: Simon & Schuster Books for Young Readers.

Diesen, Deborah, and Dan Hanna. 2008. *Pout Pout Fish*. New York: Farrar, Straus, and Giroux.

Eastman, Phillip Dey. 1961. *Go, Dog, Go*. New York: Beginner Books.

Henkes, Kevin. 1988. *Chester's Way*. New York: Greenwillow.

———. 2000. *Wemberly Worried*. New York: Greenwillow.

———. 2006. *Lilly's Purple Plastic Purse*. New York: Greenwillow.

Jenkins, Steve, and Robin Page. 2003. *What Do You Do with a Tail Like This?* Boston: Houghton Mifflin.

Kang, Anna. 2014. *You Are (Not) Small*. New York: Two Lions.

Klassen, Jon. 2011. *I Want My Hat Back*. Somerville, MA: Candlewick Press.

———. 2012. *This Is Not My Hat*. Somerville, MA: Candlewick Press.

Lionni, Leo. 1963. *Swimmy*. New York: Random House.

———. 1970. *Fish Is Fish*. New York: Random House.

Litwin, Eric. 2010. *Pete the Cat: I Love My White Shoes*. New York: Harper Collins.

Lovell, Patty. 2001. *Stand Tall, Molly Lou Melon*. New York: G.P. Putnam's Sons.

Markle, Sandra. 2014. *What If You Had Animal Hair!?* New York: Scholastic.

Martin, Bill, and Eric Carle. 1996. *Brown Bear, Brown Bear, What Do You See?* New York: Henry Holt and Co.

Novak, Benjamin Joseph. 2014. *The Book With No Pictures*. New York: Penguin Group.

O'Neill, Alexis. 2002. *The Recess Queen*. New York: Scholastic.

Petty, Dev. 2015. *I Don't Want to Be a Frog*. New York: DoubleDay Books.

Rosenthal, Amy Krouse, and Tom Lichtenheld. 2009. *Duck! Rabbit!* San Francisco: Chronicle Books.

———. 2013. *Exclamation Mark*. New York: Scholastic.

Schreiber, Anne. 2008. *Volcanoes!* Washington, D.C.: National Geographic Society.

Scieszka, John, and Lane Smith. 1996. *The True Story of the Three Little Pigs*. New York: Puffin.

Sendak, Maurice. 2012. *Where the Wild Things Are*. New York: Harper Collins.

Serafini, Frank. 2008. *Looking Closely: Across the Desert*. Toronto, ON: Kid Can Press.

———. 2008. *Looking Closely: Along the Shore*. Toronto, ON: Kids Can Press.

———. 2008. *Looking Closely: Inside the Garden*. Toronto, ON: Kid Can Press.

———. 2008. *Looking Closely: Through the Forest*. Toronto, ON: Kids Can Press.

———. 2010. *Looking Closely: Around the Pond*. Toronto, ON: Kids Can Press.

———. 2010. *Looking Closely: Into the Rainforest*. Toronto, ON: Kids Can Press.

Shannon, David. 2002. *Duck on a Bike*. New York: Blue Sky Press.

Steig, William. 1982. *Doctor De Soto*. New York. Farrar, Straus, and Giroux.

Willems, Mo. 2003. *Don't Let the Pigeon Drive the Bus!* New York: Hyperion Books.

———. 2006. *Don't Let the Pigeon Stay Up Late!* New York: Hyperion Books.

———. 2009. *Pigs Make Me Sneeze!* New York: Hyperion Books.

———. 2012. *Goldilocks and the Three Dinosaurs*. New York: Balzer + Bray.

———. 2013. *A Big Guy Took My Ball!* New York: Hyperion Books.

———. 2013. *That Is Not a Good Idea!* New York: Balzer + Bray.

———. 2014. *Waiting Is Not Easy!* New York: Hyperion Books.

———. 2015. *I Really Like Slop!* New York: Hyperion Books.